Cuba, Yes?

Cuba, Yes?

David Caute

McGraw-Hill Book Company

NEW YORK   ST. LOUIS   SAN FRANCISCO   TORONTO

Library of Congress Cataloging in Publication Data
Caute, David.
Cuba, yes?
1. Cuba—Politics and government—1959-   2. Cuba—Social
conditions. I. Title.
F1788.C33   917.291'04'64   74-2452
ISBN 0-07-010293-7

137140

Printed in the United States of America

Contents

	Preface	vii
	Prologue	1
1	Havana	15
2	More of Havana	47
3	Matanzas, Las Villas, Camagüey	87
4	Oriente	119
5	Santa Clara, Varadero, The Bay of Pigs, Pinar del Río	143
6	The Last of Havana	189

Also by David Caute

POLITICAL STUDIES
Communism and the French Intellectuals, 1914–60 (1964)
The Left in Europe since 1789 (1966)
Essential Writings of Karl Marx (edited) (1967)
Fanon (1970)
*The Fellow-Travellers: a Postscript to the
Enlightenment* (1973)

NOVELS
At Fever Pitch (1959)
Comrade Jacob (1961)
The Decline of the West (1966)
The Occupation (1971)

OTHERS
*The Illusion: an Essay on Politics, Theatre and
the Novel* (1971)
The Demonstration: A Play (1970)
Collisions. Essays and Reviews (1974)

Preface

The traveller contemplating a trip to Cuba will first examine the colour of his convictions and then the colour of his passport. Paradoxically, in view of Cuba's present political alignment, a Russian will require an entry visa whereas a British citizen, like myself, needs none. But it is the prospective American visitor to Cuba who faces real problems.

On the cover of the green American passport the gold-embossed eagle clutches in one claw a sheaf of wheat and in the other a cluster of arrows. State Department policy towards Cuba since 1960 has been all arrow and no wheat. Diplomatic relations between the two countries remain severed, and a partial economic blockade is still enforced by the US Navy. The American citizen, who nevertheless regards his own moral obligations as separate from the Navy's, will discover inside his passport the message that it is 'authorized' for travel to Cuba only 'when specifically validated for such travel by the Department of State'. (So, until recently, it went for 'Mainland China', and still goes for North Korea and North Vietnam.) But Supreme Court decisions since the late 1950s virtually immunize the traveller from retaliatory administrative action if he defies the injunction. The passport itself, without shame at self-contradiction, admits as much when it declares : 'US Courts have interpreted US law in effect on the date this passport is issued as not restricting the travel of a US citizen to any foreign country or area.'

But even if that hurdle is cleared, other obstacles will intervene. Obtaining a visa from Havana usually involves delays of two or three months before an answer, normally negative, is received. Finally, the pertinacious American who does eventually reach Cuba via Mexico City or Canada enjoys no direct consular protection other than that of the Swiss Government where it acts as a stand-in. There are several reasons for Cuban obduracy. Nations, like individuals, fall quickly into the attitude of 'If you won't speak to me, I won't speak to you.' It is also the case that for more than ten years the CIA has been attempting to flood Cuba with its own agents. Although most of them are, or were, Cuban nationals, the régime in Havana remains crouched in suspicion of any American visitor whose political credentials are other than impeccable.

Impeccable, for example, are the credentials of the young volunteers of the American Venceremos Brigade who visit Cuba in batches of one or two hundred at a time. In 1964 a relatively large contingent of American journalists was accorded a warm welcome by Castro, but freedom of movement and investigation is more typically granted to correspondents whom Fidel has reason to trust, like Herbert Matthews of the *New York Times*. Disaffected radicals like Stokely Carmichael have also been welcome. Otherwise, a high proportion of American visitors have been involuntary ones who, having planned to spend a week with Aunt Mary in Florida, have found themselves hijacked to within inches of Fidel's barbarous beard. (In Cuba, the much-loved bearded guerrillas are known as '*los barbudos*'.)

And yet before 1959 the American was Cuba's most familiar visitor, virtually dominating as he did large areas of Cuban economic and political life. We shall discover that the legacy of that shattering impact is still visible in Cuba, just as British, French, or Spanish influence remains apparent even in former colonies which have vigorously rejected the metropolitan power. That Americans will return to Cuba, I have no doubt. But how soon? If Nixon can achieve an understanding, a working relationship, with godless Communist China, for twenty years the fount of evil in the American consciousness, surely the same *Realpolitik* is possible with regard to a small island of seven million people situated only ninety-eight miles from the Florida shore? The mutual agreement of 1973 to discourage hijacking is a first step.

Whether or not many Americans would welcome the chance to spend a vacation in Castro's Cuba is another matter. The European is always surprised by the virulence, the emotional intensity, of American anti-Communism. I happened to be in New York in September 1960 when Castro and Khrushchev were visiting the United Nations and shaking Manhattan to its foundations. (Castro, you may recall, took his delegation to stay in the Hotel Theresa in Harlem.) Hatred and hysteria sizzled off the burning sidewalks. I remember walking past the Castro convertible furniture store and wondering how it could afford to maintain its name. Even to the sympathetic and admiring foreigner, American society may appear paranoiacally racked by fear and suspicion. As citizen, voter, newspaper-reader, TV-observer, Rotarian, Legionnaire, and churchman, the American appears to be unusually susceptible to rumour of devils and discovery of witches. Communism, represented as the universal satanic force of our time, as the atheistical, materialist conspiracy which will stop at nothing to achieve its hideous design of world domination, as the evil doctrine dedicated to abolishing the family, 'nationalizing women' and brainwashing children, was the viper at the bottom of almost every American's bed. And Fidel Castro turned out to be, or became, a Communist. As a result, it was assumed that this flamboyant and rhetorical young man threatened the whole edifice of American power and prosperity.

It would be futile to deny that the majority of North Americans tend to ignore their neighbours to the south or to dismiss them as politically volatile and immature. From Seattle to Charleston little sleep is lost over the cruel and reactionary Latin American despotisms which resolve class-conflicts by means of murder and which, with the support of interested North American corporations, maintain the bulk of the peasant population in a condition of economic dependence akin to slavery. (Not that Americans are the only affluent people who eat oranges and bananas without a second thought; I remember a London barrow-boy answering my query as to whether his oranges came from South Africa with the angry retort that fruit picked by 'niggers' was fine if you could peel off the skin.) The North American tends to awaken to Latin American problems only when there is 'trouble'—which, as his mass media take care to assure him, involves the naked theft of legitimate American property. But the mass media, of course, are tied to shareholders and advertisers who may well be tied to the stolen property. The greater and most influential part of the American Press (as we shall see later) has persistently depicted the Havana régime in the most disparaging, if not diabolical, terms. And yet ... was not the same true of China? And is it not the case that today many Americans, loyal citizens and God-fearing churchgoers, are eagerly awaiting the chance to visit China? The paradox of the American personality is the co-existence of fierce enmity towards certain categories of foreigner with the latent fund of goodwill, with that ineradicable desire to love and be loved, which climaxes in the warmest, most vigorous handshake in the world. (Witness only the warm reception accorded to Khrushchev in the Ohio farmlands in 1959.)

Of course, a diplomatic agreement, a normalization of relations, carries dangers for both sides. Cuba is Communist and Cuba is close; she speaks, or aspires to speak, to all of

Latin America, and the hostility of most Latin American Governments is a false indicator of popular sentiment throughout the continent. For America, Cuba remains the thorn in the flesh, the potential poisoned source of an escalating subversion of American capital and American influence. Containing Cuba is rather like holding a cork in a champagne bottle—either a firm hand or pop! Would concession imply capitulation? It is not clear. Diplomacy is always a gamble in psychology. Concession could also involve castration, a cunning emasculation of Cuba's fire-eating posture, a wooing-away from Soviet influence, a sly invitation to the table of respectability. In the short term one cannot predict the outcome. Meanwhile, the winds which blow across the Caribbean and the Gulf of Mexico will remain stormy.

Cuba, Yes?

Prologue

I am an unrepentant daydreamer.

This is the last day before our departure. I am wandering up and down Oxford Street, picking my passage between the fruit-barrows, the balloon-peddlers, and the trinket-vendors, in a drowsy effort to equip myself for the great expedition. In the modish, unisex clothes-shops which spring up in London like mushrooms, staffed by emaciated, unisex youths, I search vainly for elegant hot-country gear which will allow me to breathe, protect my sun-shy neck and forearms, be easy to wash, and leave a little money over for the sleeping pills, pep pills, anti-mosquito cream, stomach pills, razor blades, and rolls of Kodak I must buy in Boots the Chemists. Time passes but I have made no purchases; everything is either too tight at the chest or too long in the leg. I am about to make despairingly for that reliable but unfashionable general store, Marks & Spencer's, when I hear a droning in the blue sky overhead. A great steel bird is majestically turning for its westerly descent to Heathrow Airport; head tilted up, I stand and gape ...

... I pick my moment according to the manual: four minutes after take-off, heading for the English Channel, with the fuselage beginning to level off at ten thousand feet. The 'fasten seat-belts' sign has been extinguished, and I am quite unimpeded as I stride up the aisle towards the cockpit, unobtrusively clad in beard, green fatigues, and forage cap, my eyes masked by dark lenses, a folded hammock slung across my shoulder, a machete dangling from my ammunition belt, Che Guevara's thoughts on guerrilla warfare clasped lightly in my head, and a rifle in my hand. A jutting cigar precedes me—me, disciple of Fidel, beloved colleague of Che, survivor of the Moncada Barracks fiasco, veteran of the *Granma*, hero of the Sierra Maestra, and later clandestine *comandante* in a hundred wars of liberation from the Congo to Bolivia. The Man, in short, the CIA Most Want to Find Dead or Alive. Brushing a couple of stewardesses aside, I am confronted by a bullish steward; he crumples from a blow he never saw. (We know our way around, *compañero*.) I enter the control cabin, my thumb resting meaningfully on a cargo of death.

'Make it Havana,' I snap.

'*Havana?*' The pilot looks unhappy.

'Havana, Cuba. Cuba, *si! Patria o muerte! Venceremos!* Fidel, *el jefe máximo*, expects me, get it? Come now, *gusano* of imperialism, turn your plane, the Revolution is its own clock and I am not afraid to die.'

Suddenly, I receive a heavy jolt between the shoulder blades. A stranger is surveying me sceptically.

'Sorry, mate. But if you will block the pavement ...'

I hurry across the street to Marks & Spencer's and purchase a pair of cotton pants one can climb in and out of without unstitching the seams.

That night, as I toss in bed, possessed by the adventure ahead (Oh Cuba, symbol of justice, small island of fire and ferment), my wife sleeps with insensitive nonchalance. At seven a.m. she cheerfully pulls me out of bed.

'You don't look good,' she says, hurrying me into my clothes and pouring coffee down my throat. When the last key has been turned, the last label tied, and the last zip zipped, I begin to play Hamlet with my electric razor.

2

'Shall I take it after all?'

'I thought we had resolved that.'

'But you know how my skin cuts up with blades. And suppose there isn't hot water?'

'Well what did you do in the Sierra Maestra?' I wilt. 'Besides,' she adds, 'we're overweight already.' She taps my pockets.

'Passports?'

'Yes.'

'Traveller's cheques?'

'Yes.'

'Then it's time to leave.'

'It occurs to me that we may need some form of rainwear. I daresay you imagine that Cuba is an oven of uninterrupted sun, but if you study the weather charts you'll discover that at this time of year ...'

'I bought two fold-up plastic macs yesterday.'

She leads me down to the waiting taxi. *Compañero*, these women of the new generation will leave us nothing of our *machismo*.

In the taxi she gives me a small white tablet to swallow.

'What is it?'

'Swallow it.'

At the airport we stock up with duty-free cigarettes and Martha buys the *Guardian* and *Newsweek*. Over coffee I make a show of studying the Spanish phrase-book.

'And what,' I ask, 'is the Spanish for "thank you very much"?'

'*Muchas gracias.*'

'Really, your pronunciation. *Moo-chas grá-thee-as.*'

'I thought the Latin Americans pronounced the "c" softly, as in "ceramics".'

'Do they?'

'You're the one with the book.'

'What's the difference between *adiós* and *hasta la vista*?'

'The first one is more final.'

Desperately I turn the pages. 'What's "it's love-fifteen"? I'll tell you: *estamos a cero a quince.* Or how about, "I want two prints of each negative". God, I hope we brought enough film; you do realize film is unobtainable over there or only fits Soviet cameras or something like that?'

She snatches the book from me. 'Count from one to ten,' she commands.

I stumble on 'six'.

'*Seis*,' she says sternly. '*Say-ees*.'

'*Say-ees*.'

'Again.'

I snatch the phrase-book back: 'I bet you can't do, "Would passengers on Flight 10 to Barcelona please go to door A".'

Martha buries her nose in the *Guardian* where there is news of Fischer and Spassky in Reykjavik. She and I have so far failed to get our own twenty-four-match tournament off the ground because we both insist on being Boris rather than Bobby.

Our plane is announced: Flight BE 621 to Prague. The passengers assemble at gate eleven. A group of well-fed Czechoslovak businessmen are chatting quietly in a language I don't understand. We shuffle forward towards the exit and I wonder why it is I can never sleep the night before any unusual event, be it even that I have had to set the alarm clock.

'Are you carrying a gun?'

Amazed, I blink. A spruce young steward in a blue uniform is regarding me with the utmost dispassion. I gawp then grin, but his scrutiny is unwavering. 'Do you speak English?' he inquires.

'Yes.'

'Are you carrying a gun?'

'No.'

'Please raise your arms.'

4

He frisks me with the nimble fingers of a tailor measuring the inside of the leg. My wife, who has escaped with a ridiculously cursory glance into her purse, averts her eyes politely, as if disparaging the inevitability of my gunlessness.

Fasten seat-belts, please. Sir, the back of your seat should be in an upright position for take-off. Glancing around, I take note of the almost laboured boredom plastered on the features of my fellow-passengers: all awe, all anticipation, anaesthetized. For my own part, as the Trident trundles to the end of the runway, puffs its soaring lungs, and explodes into motion, I am consumed by childlike excitement, by the mysteries of geography and by the ancient magnetic stone of discovery. Climbing with regulation-softened engines, the Trident turns over Windsor Castle and the neat red rows of suburban semi-detached houses which stretch out from London in a relentless expansion of polluted air. Cuba! Land of the heroic guerrilla, epicentre of revolt, Caribbean dagger thrust close to the belly of Florida, at last, after all these years of dreaming and planning and talking and reading, at last I am coming! My wife's fingers slip through my own: we both feel a huge question-mark beginning to bend within us.

Since this book describes a journey I may legitimately pause to speculate about the nature, the quality, of modern travel. We creatures of the jet age have, I suspect, allowed a banal pseudo-sophistication to dull the sense of awe and wonder which possessed the nineteenth-century traveller. Raging seas, deserts of death, malarial, tiger-infested jungles, hostile tribesmen—all are now shrunk to the puny proportions of a plasticine model by the atmospheric arrogance of the flying machine. (Admittedly the hostile tribesmen may hijack the plane.) Mr W. H. Auden once wrote: 'It is impossible to take a train or an aeroplane without having a fantasy of oneself as a Quest Hero setting off in search of an enchanted princess on the Waters of Life.' Impossible for how many of us? Scarcely deigning to glance out of the oval window at the revolving globe, we smoke, cocktail, lunch, and magazine our suave trajectory above the clouds, erecting inner barriers to what is strange, foreign, different. Indeed, we demand that the worldwide tourist industry should constantly minimize the strains of adjustment with cola and a hot shower in the middle of the African bush, an air-conditioned, Hilton-style view of the great falls, and by the universal power of the dollar. Let every disturbing local custom be ironed out into the utilitarian shape of a foldable globe-kit and let there be ice in our whisky—everywhere. We scan catalogues in search of guaranteed sea-and-sunshine, acceptable package terms for room and board, scarcely caring whether the natives speak Spanish, Dutch, or Swahili, because if they know what's good for them they'll speak enough serviceable English to meet our needs. (And kindly don't serve any dubious foreign dishes.)

We are tourists, not travellers. The tourist in his air-conditioned bus, cocooned in his hygienic capsule, is essentially a man or woman on the defensive, protected from alien hearts, alien smells, alien tongues. His movie-camera, in one respect a sign of an unquenchable curiosity, also represents the urge to capture and tame by means of dispassionate gadgetry the great, ragged, anthill of the heaving world.

Perhaps we are in too much of a hurry: each one a private time-and-motion study, grudgingly measuring distances in jet-hours rather than as the delicate unfolding of a transient consciousness. We know where we are going and to hell with everything in between. To arrive in Mexico three cocktails after leaving New York is to misapprehend Mexico and to inflict violence on our faculties of adaptation and assimilation. It is perhaps because we feel cheated by our newly acquired invulnerability that we react to news of air disasters with fascination as well as horror. The machine suddenly fails, gravity laughs, and we spin through the sky into the web of our ancestors. Stranded on a remote mountain, the survivors begin to eat the dead. The image of that mountain peak awaiting its chance (our electronic error) to deal us a staggering blow suggests an elemental retribution for man's defiance of his natural limitations, his *hubris*. But in the face of such dangers we meanly snatch little insurance cards from painted dispensers.

Of course, the spirit of exploration is not dead in a few privileged spirits; there are still genuine travellers, hitch-hikers, madyachtsmen, tentfamilies, and crazycyclists abroad on the oceans and highways. And even within the confines of a package tour you will find some who are anchored to the timetable while others are always beavering to create private spaces in which to beat their own trail. The most that the majority of us can hope to be is one of the latter.

The clouds part to reveal gentle, cultivated fields rising beneath us. A few moments later we touch down at Prague and the Czechoslovak businessmen heave a collectivized sigh of contentment. You may well wonder why one should travel from London to Havana via Prague, which is manifestly in the wrong direction, but such geographical gymnastics can be explained only in terms of the perverse state of the world. In Europe there are only three points of embarkation for Cuba, one in the West (Madrid) and two in the East (Prague and Moscow). Whereas the last two can be understood in terms of current political alliances, the Madrid connection represents not only Spain's desire to maintain influences in her former New World colonies, but also those cultural and linguistic bonds which—sometimes —transcend political enmities. It so happens, however, that the French agency which has organized our tour has an

7

arrangement with Czechoslovak Airlines, thus bringing me back, full of misgivings, to a beautiful city I learned to love deeply in the brave liberal spring of 1968. The airport, I notice, has been completely modernized since the Warsaw Pact armies arrived one night in August 1968 to save socialism; no doubt the Red Army found the toilet facilities inadequate, the immigration officials lax, and the workshops poorly equipped to repair tanks.

My wife and I have two-way transit visas.

Beyond the Customs counter F—— is standing, waving gaily, gesturing, grimacing, welcoming us as if nothing had happened, as if he had not recently been deprived of his job and forced to depend on the generosity of his grown-up children. It is this gentle, compassionate and creative man, let me say, who truly embodies 'socialism with a human face'—and not the hard-jawed *Hintermänner*, stooges, time-servers, ventriloquists, and yesmen who once again consign all independent voices to prison by way of rigid trials. And F—— does, after a decent interval, after absorbing the warmth in our breath, permit himself to sigh. To sigh for the microphones in the walls, the tapped telephone, the purges and excommunications, the closed theatres, the banned periodicals, to sigh for the season of decency which had flourished four years before. To sigh for physicists building roads, philosophers cleaning lavatories, writers silenced —in short, for all these 'enemies of socialism' who have been thoroughly unmasked and justly punished.

I ask to see the Old Town Square again, particularly as Martha, who is greatly interested in the art and architecture of Central Europe, has never seen it. The house of Franz Kafka, the mellow stones and finely variegated pastel shades, the crazy roofs and irregular windows of Old Europe—this is the only environment in which I feel truly at home. The sobriety in the air, and the continuity; the role of nuance and the violin. The old Jewish cemetery, with its mildewed stones keeling over from the force of geology and human brutality, the Old-New Synagogue with its tray of skull-caps, its golden candelabra, and its ageing remnant of survivors.

F—— is now without a passport, without work, without a future, but somehow he has managed to salvage his little French car which he squeezes between the sidewalks and the street cars, screeching his tyres on the cobbles and talking calmly of the men in raincoats who shadow his movements. In the stately Slavia Hotel opposite the National Theatre we are served coffee by black-coated waiters, as if nothing had happened; and the faces of the people in the streets, this civilized race whose fate always is to be crushed between predatory giants, are also without trace of Dubček's disgrace, of Jan Palach's saintly suicide. In American parlance, Prague has once again been 'pacified'. We return to F——'s house for dinner, where we meet again his family and other old friends. The two of us, so privileged by the accident of birth, quietly absorb a nightmare related with stoical forti-tude. So we are on our way to Cuba? They are interested in Cuba and wonder what it will be like. We promise to tell them on the return journey.

F—— drives us to the airport and my Anglo, lawn-conscious eye notices the untended couch grass at the road-side, the Continent's last manifestation of civic irresponsi-bility. We say goodbye to F—— and sit down to wait. At five in the evening we are shunted along corridors and down stairs to a small hall through the windows of which we can see several aircraft refuelling and loading luggage. Corralled here behind locked doors, and periodically counted by blue-eyed stewardesses of Czechoslovak Airlines, there is no alternative but to appraise one's fellow-travellers, the majority of whom seem to be French, Dutch, and Swiss. Now is the first opportunity to reckon compatibility, to fasten on possible companions, to tag the ogres one must avoid. The

9

initial impression, we both agree, is disconcertingly geriatric and juvenile, a motley collection of grandparents and youths, whereas we—you understand—are poised in the prime of life where energy and maturity are perfectly fused, where promise has turned to achievement, where power remains compatible with beauty. It slowly dawns on me that we have by no means volunteered for a company of heroic guerrillas willing to brave snakes, scorpions, mosquitoes, and hostile American surveillance in the cause of universal liberation, but, rather—the impression is inescapable—a bunch of eccentrics. Of nuts. Are we, too, nuts? What sane man would squander his hard-earned annual vacation in an ostracized island still subject to food-rationing? I glance at Martha. She is calm and perversely inscrutable. My eyes, reverting to their haphazard search-and-destroy mission, are diverted by some elegant examples of the *jeunesse dorée*, those lithe, supple, bronzed children of the sun who crowd the Mediterranean beaches and play volleyball with expensive handkerchiefs pinned round their loins; young men in necklaces and girls whose narcissism is interrupted only by a few snatched hours of sleep. Well!—how commendable that they should now dedicate themselves to more serious things and commit their energies to the Third World. This illusion, however, is not destined to endure for long; these joyful creatures, it will later emerge, are heading for the Cuban beachcamp at Jibacoa, where they will lie in the sun for three weeks.

Suddenly the exit doors open and there is a stampede across the tarmac: the survival of the fittest. Martha and I take to our heels, knocking aside the old and infirm, and grab two comfortable seats in the centre of the big Soviet-built Ilyushin. The row of seats in front of us, aligned to an emergency exit, has been removed, allowing us to stretch our legs during the night ahead. Purring with selfish contentment, we settle back and play spectator to the throng of anxious latecomers pushing their way down the central aisle in search of vacant seats. On so precariously international an expedition as this, minor errors of calculation are far from minor for the last man on board.

Happily, there is a place for everyone. The huge aircraft subsides into a symphony of grunts, clicks, and shufflings. At this point Kafka makes his entrance in the shape of a stout Czechoslovak Airlines official who insists that a seat number is written on our boarding cards and that we are all therefore wrongly seated. Couples and families, re-examining their cards, now discover that they have been scattered throughout the plane, possibly on the principle that in the event of a crash each family will provide a survivor to identify dead kinsfolk. The official finally recoils from his duty in the face of overwhelming passive resistance. From all quarters arises an audible sigh of relief.

Our sky-blue hostesses offer us sweets and smiles. We lift off smoothly. It is dusk and Cuba is twelve hours away.

Martha extracts a small chess-set from her bag. We rest it on the arm of the seat, slot the minuscule rooks and pawns into their holes with fingers suddenly fat and clumsy, and settle down to the Battle of the Atlantic. An hour after take-off we pass over London.

Night infiltrates the windows prematurely, advanced by our westerly rush. Our fellow-passengers have now been overtaken by sleep and Martha's queen, quite dead, squats scowling beyond the ropes, willing her careless mistress to deal me a blow below the belt of my *machismo*. As the engines lapse into a gentle hum and the nose of the plane dips down towards Gander, Newfoundland, I make my inevitable careless move, then hastily retract.

'No.'

'What do you mean, "no"?'

'You took your hand off the piece.'

'Only for a split second.'

But her gaze is a Supreme Court and I shrug in sulky resignation.

'Do take it back if you want to,' she says.

As we walk across the tarmac at Gander, the air is dry and crisp, the last salute of the Northern Hemisphere. For an hour we idle among the crowded magazine-racks and wander from the cafeteria to the bar while the big Ilyushin soaks in fuel beside a friendly, maple-leafed Canadian fighter. (The Canadians have always been reluctant Cold Warriors.) As we lift off again and head southwards, parallel to the Eastern Seaboard of the United States, fatigue closes my eyes and my thoughts scatter along a gallery of sleeping American friends. (In fact, our Czech pilot maintains a respectful distance from Uncle Sam's fiercely patrolled shore.) Then all consciousness dims.

'Did you sleep?'

Martha is shaking me.

'I must have. Did you?'

'I thought you wouldn't want to miss breakfast.'

Growing fresher and brighter-eyed by the hour, our hostesses are distributing trays laden with cheese, salami, black olives, and cake. I recoil from the food and reach out for the hot coffee. Already passengers are beginning to form a queue outside the toilets as though this were their last chance for three weeks. Tension invades me like a gas. I stretch, yawn, and shake myself.

The first sip of hot coffee revives me. Cuba! Cuba! For how many years have I sworn to make this holy pilgrimage to the new Mecca of permanent revolution, how I have loved, cherished, and admired you, and now, rising up from the south, you are almost upon me! *But what are you really like?*

With shaking hands I reach for the phrase-book. I have only a few minutes to master every conceivable facet of grammar and vocabulary.

'What's "I'm very sorry"?'

'*Lo siento mucho.*'

'What's "he is a pansy"?'

'I thought they had abolished pansies.'

'Well, you never know.'

I close the book and my eyes as well. Columbus had called it the fairest isle he ever saw ... somewhere below, the ships of the US Navy prowl ... that famous photograph of Che in Bolivia, dead, gazed upon contemptuously by a well-dressed officer ... posters of Che for sale in Soho and the East Village ... Castro in Moscow in a fur hat ... girls of the militia in khaki mini-skirts strutting through Havana ... Fidel lecturing white-shirted prisoners after the Bay of Pigs ... the Missile Crisis ... the star in Che's beret ... Fidel cutting cane ... no prostitutes now ... Cuba, isolated and ostracized, boycotted by its West Indian neighbours, at loggerheads with Haiti and the Dominican Republic, fortress Cuba fed and fuelled by the Soviet merchant marine ...

'How much longer?' I ask a passing stewardess. She breaks stride and tilts her head. '*Wann kommen wir an, bitte?*'

'*Etwa dreissig Minuten.*'

I turned to Martha. 'Which of the world's airlines call at Havana? Please write legibly and on one side of the paper only.'

'Iberia, Aeroflot, and these people ... Is there another? I know, Air Cubana!'

Quite right. The Mexicans lean both ways, tolerating two flights a week to Havana but appeasing the United States by stamping the traveller's passport to the effect that he has visited Cuba. Leper.

Martha wants a second cup of coffee and so do I, with or without the powdered, unlactiferous substance airlines call milk. The stewardess, proudly holding an empty coffee jug, flashes me a smile of promise. And suddenly the big Ilyushin dips its nose, the engines relax and we begin our descent. My wife's cool fingers coil through my own and squeeze gently.

Havana.

CHAPTER

I

Havana

The words JOSE MARTI AIRPORT are blocked out in big, red-neon capitals above the terminal building. But the T is out of order. Wilting in the damp heat, we straggle towards a single rectangle of light through an impression of emptiness. Our Ilyushin seems to be the only plane in sight. We enter a small utility room where a girl in a striped frock is distributing long forms which turn out to be question-naires. As we read through these the mood among our party is one of mounting astonishment. A very old French lady, whom we will later come to know all too well as Madame Bourgeois, is wailing her confusion and trepidation. She doesn't understand Spanish. Nicole, our sleek French guide, calmly points out to her that the questions are also printed in French, as well as English. Ashen-white, with violently rouged cheeks and wearing a beige hat with a huge pin which seems to run right through her skull, mean-featured, jackal-eyed, and clutching an enormous purse, Madame Bourgeois sits down with a snort and declares in sharp Parisian tones: 'It's ridiculous.'

Question: Do you know any Cubans living abroad? If so, whom, when, where, and why? *Question*: Are you an entrepreneur, landowner, or employer? If so, how, where, and why? *Question*: What political and social organizations do you belong to in your own country?

I nudge Martha, who looks distinctly nonplussed. 'It's the Isle of Pines for you, baby.'

'What's that?'

'It's where they keep the political prisoners.'

While we are lining up to show our passports, two girls distribute delicious iced-lemon drinks and four male musicians welcome us with local songs. But I am brooding. The interrogatory enthusiasm represented by this questionnaire certainly puts the US Immigration Service in the shade. Does Cuba have its own Attorney General's list? Will the completed forms be filed with the House Un-Cuban Activities Committee? (No: contemporary Cuba doesn't have the benefit of a House of Representatives.) It's true that, in Boston, Massachusetts, I once attended a meeting of the Fair Play for Cuba Committee, in the course of which young patriots threw eggs at the eminent and much harassed advocate of international reconciliation, Professor Linus Pauling, but I'm damned if I'm going to write that down. I abscond with a second glass of lemon, which we share between us.

'What shall we write?' Martha wants to know.

'Put down the following: member of Chamber of Commerce, Daughter of the American Revolution, affiliate of Catholic War Veterans, Rotarian, Kiwani, dupe, stooge, fellow-traveller of capitalist-front organizations. In short, CapSymp.'

'I'm going to sign my name and leave the rest blank.'

One of our party, a tall fellow with flaxen hair, a milky skin and a large stomach, carrying an American Express bag over his shoulder, taps me on the shoulder.

'You from England?' he says in English.

'That's right.'

'This is all crap,' he says, slapping the questionnaire and

moving away. (Our first encounter with the Young Swiss.)

Our passports are removed. We shall not see them again until our departure.

'How do we cash traveller's cheques without passports?' Martha asks Nicole.

'There's no problem,' the French girl says.

We meet up with our suitcases, disgorged from the belly of the aeroplane, and feel slightly reassured. A black Customs man invites us to open them in words which refuse to commit themselves to any particular language. He probes the contents. He goes on probing, opening, untying, feeling, squeezing, examining. Nothing is too private for his gentle fingers. He confiscates our apples and oranges, but they do the same in England. He carries away our shoes and slippers and dips them in disinfectant. The guitarist is strumming happily and the singers are serenading us into Cuba as the customs man turns his attention to serious business—our books. The Spanish phrase-book and the pocket dictionary are OK: he returns them.

'What's the phrase for "please don't confiscate my phrase-book"?' I mutter.

He picks up a Penguin edition of *Fidel Castro*, by Castro's friend, Herbert Matthews. He sets it aside. He examines cursorily *Havana Journal*, an entirely sympathetic account of the January 1968 Cultural Congress by the Jamaican novelist Andrew Salkey (with whom I periodically chat at various demonstrations, occupations, and sit-ins against imperialism). This book is also set aside. Ditto a collection of Cuban short stories originally written and published in Revolutionary Cuba but—fatally—translated and republished in London. Next, our censor lifts a volume of speeches by none other than Fidel Castro; alas, they are in French, with an introduction by an independent editor, and so they too are set aside. Meanwhile, there is evidence of unrest and distress to the right and left of us as our fellow-passengers

17

undergo similar expropriations. A young man who is studying architecture loses an expensive study of post-Revolutionary Cuban architecture written by an architect who
remains in high favour in Havana, but, fatally, translated
into English and published in London. (Later the Cuban
architect will replace our friend's volume with a more up-to-
date one.) A Hollander groans as he says goodbye to Che
Guevara's *Bolivian Diary* translated into Dutch.

We watch the pile of confiscated books grow, horrified.
What are we going to read during the long, empty evenings
ahead? I have been in Russia, Yugoslavia, Czechoslovakia,
and East Germany, but nothing like this has ever happened
before. One brings particular books to a particular country
because they will assume greater urgency and relevance in
the environment they describe, and because one wants to
measure one's own observations against those of others.

Our man now lightly lifts Graham Greene's novel, *Our
Man in Havana*. I shrug in resignation. But, to my surprise,
he returns it to me. Abruptly I understand: it deals
exclusively with pre-Revolutionary Cuba, with Havana in
the time of Batista. Flaubert and Trollope, whom we
snatched haphazardly from the shelves of unread books
moments before our departure, also prove acceptable. With
a nod we are informed that we may now lock our cases.
The Customs official carries away our books, neatly tied with
a label bearing our name, into an office. Possessed by rage,
I confront Nicole.

'What kind of a farce is this?'

'They will be examined by a commission,' she replies
calmly, 'and later returned to you.'

'When?'

'It varies.'

'What are they afraid of?'

'It's the new policy.'

'New since when?'

'Since last year.'

'But what are they afraid of? A few books, mainly in foreign languages...'

'There has been trouble in the past.'

'What kind of trouble?'

She shrugs, declining to indicate whether she herself is in the dark or whether, alternatively, I have no right to penetrate the Revolution's necessary strategies of self-preservation. As she turns abruptly away, dismissively, I utter my first counter-revolutionary remark. I am still brooding as we cash traveller's cheques and receive in exchange a toy currency which is valueless outside Cuba. The official exchange rate, which equates the peso with the dollar, merely milks the tourist: the black-market rate of four pesos to the dollar more closely reflects actual values, and the currency black market, after all, is merely the stock exchange gone underground. The Cubans, like the Russians, have a great fear of the black market, and the cashier severely enjoins us to keep all our receipts for presentation at the time of departure. But this is mere bluff and can be disregarded with impunity.

On the coach into Havana we meet our Cuban guide, Carlos. He is a light, agile black, aged thirty, very friendly and interested in his new charges. He speaks good French but little English. I ask him about the confiscated books and he shrugs apologetically.

'I hope they will be delivered to your hotel quite soon.'

'But why are they taken away?'

'Well, you know, in Cuba we have many problems.'

We pass along empty, darkened streets. Half an hour later we reach the Hotel Deauville, overlooking the sea, are assigned modern, comfortable rooms with rapid efficiency, and fall exhausted into bed. It is now two a.m. Cuban (and New York) time, seven a.m. London time. The air-conditioning in our room doesn't work, but a large jug of iced water is welcome. We are situated on the eighth floor and pray for a cool breeze from the sea, but the air is like a sponge cake and we toss naked on top of the sheets in search of sleep.

'We forgot to use the mosquito cream,' Martha says softly.

'Yes, we did.' A moment later I have drifted into a light, restless sleep packed with harassing dreams having nothing to do with Cuba or our journey.

The inner clock is now protesting, hauling me back into consciousness limb by limb, jabbing needles into my head, coating my eyes with acid. I drag myself to the window and peer resentfully at the rooftops of Havana, the waterfront and the Malecon. An image of Riverside Drive and the Hudson River lodges for a moment, then evaporates. I crawl back under the sheet. Martha is tossing painfully like a woman in labour. I twiddle the knob of the bedside radio, pick up a voice, *guajira* music, another voice, then an opera. Reaching the bathroom I plunge my hand into the washbag hoping for the best. There is no hot water, and after a short encounter with a razor blade I emerge with a face ravaged by Dracula. There is a semblance of a sympathetic moan from the tormented creature in the other bed. Aching from head to toe, we descend eight floors and enter a streamlined dining-room replete with white table-cloths and waiters in black bow-ties. Of our fellow-travellers there is no sign. Are we the first or the last to face the day? A waiter is brushing breadcrumbs off an adjoining table: we are the last. The coffee is good, but the waiters grow a bit restive when we demand a fifth helping.

Gingerly we step out into the street. The sky is cloudy and the air humid, sultry, oppressive, laden with an aroma of seaweed which I first mistake for sewage. Outside the hotel a crowd of children besieges us, demanding cigarettes, chewing-gum, biro pens, and any pesos which may be

damaging our pockets. Without a map, we point ourselves
haphazardly towards rising domes and spires and begin our
way along sidewalks pitted and broken like bear-traps,
pursued all the while by ragged urchins, whose mothers
observe our tormented progress placidly from upper
windows and doorsteps. Buckets dangle on ropes outside
the tenements, old men are playing chess in the shadows,
and there is an overwhelming impression of dilapidation.
Then one old character, perhaps drunk, perhaps clobbered
by the passing years, waylays us with reminiscences of the
good old days in Miami. He wants cigarettes and I give him
too many—I haven't yet dropped anchor in this country.

One does not expect to encounter beggars in contemporary
Cuba, and indeed one normally does not. But the area round
the Deauville Hotel is populated by displaced lumpen
proletarians who seize the opportunity when it arises—not
out of desperation or destitution, but from old habit. These
people, as Carlos will later explain, are unreconstructed
for the time being, but plans are afoot to transform them
into good citizens. For some tourists, squatting beggars
imbue an old city with charm, but I am not of that per-
suasion. The beggar merely imposes on me an unwelcome
appraisal of myself, my good clean clothes, my well-heeled
shoes, my bulging pockets, my camera, my pale, unsunned
face sheltering from guilt under a protective brim. One can,
of course, take refuge in mild indignation; the beggar is the
victim of his own indigence or the demon drink or a
morally rotten society. It follows that one's own relative
affluence is the result of crucifying labour and stern dedication to duty. But I am not so persuaded.

Nor is the choice pleasant. To give to one is to encourage
the others; whereupon you either empty your pockets or
resort to an ugly display of anger. Yet to pass by, eyes fixed
resolutely ahead, as if this human being's diminished dignity
deserved only scorn, is certainly to inflict a small wound

upon oneself. The third solution, to distinguish the authentic beggar from the pushing opportunist, involves a process of scrutiny and judgment so invidious as to be intolerable. And so it goes. But Castro's Cuba is without genuine beggars.

Martha points out a 'socialist emulation' sticker on a boarded-up shop window. So many shops are boarded up. Some carry announcements of forthcoming events, parades and demonstrations, others are lacquered in portraits of Fidel. In 1968 the Revolution abruptly turned against the urban petty-bourgeoisie, the small shopkeepers and restaurant-owners, and sent them packing on the pretext that they were technically employers hiring labour and motivated by profit. So here, as we walk away from the sea up the Avenue Italia towards the Avenue Simon Bolívar, the Revolution announces a space, a desolation, a clearing-away, but offers no replacement, no compensatory act of urban creation.

Sunday. Men, idle, loitering at street corners, silently heckling pretty girls with that Latin truculence which is achieved only within the immunity of the group. They stand outside buildings which are peeling and shabby, but also clean and wholesome; buildings which attest to an exhausting war, to rationing and austerity and sacrifice, but not to degeneration or despair.

Soon I am getting tired of being watched, of slowly swivelling eyes; of course it is not *my* legs which attract their stares, their mutual nudges, their laughing remarks, but some kind of judgment on me is implied, vaguely derisive, as if I must be a cuckold to let her display so much flesh to the world. I dislike being an object of attention, even secondary attention, in public.

Martha's short skirts were also a focus of attention in the streets of Siberia, but there the contours of the problem were different and, to me, more acceptable. At a distance of fifty yards an approaching male would assess this foreign temptation advancing upon him and then, mindful of Soviet dignity and all that he had been taught as a Young Pioneer, hurry past with upturned gaze, as if searching for sputniks. It was the gaggles of old women in their aprons and peasant scarves who would stop, turn, stare and mutter reproachfully. That annoyed me less; the superstitious strictures of the old weather-beaten hags were directed purely at the brazen hussy who, if she had been a daughter of theirs... But when we penetrated the southerly regions of Uzbekistan, where men sit together in the long shadows of their Moslem heritage, the reactions became disturbingly aggressive. About clothes the Cubans are somewhat uptight; after lunch Carlos will enjoin the men in our party on no account to venture into city streets wearing shorts or sandals.

'For Christ's sake, why?'

'You will be taken for a homosexual.'

'Because of a pair of sandals?'

'And shorts also.'

'And supposing one is a homosexual?'

'The Revolution is attempting to eradicate the pederasts.'

'Why?'

'They are anti-social.'

And the truth is, the homosexuals of Cuba have been foully hounded, persecuted. Even in modern Cuban short stories the evil characters, the traitors, the spies, the 'Batistianos', tend to be homosexuals.

We are wandering aimlessly, still aching from our journey, and our feet are hot. Old American cars of the 1950s, held together by ingenuity and willpower, groaning under the load of family outings, head out of town. The drivers, when unaccompanied by their womenfolk, sound their horns at passing female pedestrians—an intermittent honk-honk of ritual *machismo*. Children are playing in the squares, but there is no breeze today and their little kites refuse to fly. The buses are crowded, the shops empty or boarded up. In this city which was once an international playground, we cannot find a café or a bar in which to sit down and drink. But the sign 'Sloppy Joe's', immortalized in Greene's *Our Man in Havana*, catches my eye above a boarded-up bar.

The city of Havana on a Sunday morning. The sun immobilizes, but so does underdevelopment. Castro constantly harangues his people about this: you are brave in crises, he says, and you know how to die a hero's death, but you are lacking in steady industry and perseverance. At first the people are happy to learn that the Revolution, their Revolution, is directed against the rich, the landowners, the landlords, the bosses. In time, that victory is won. But the leader, *el jefe máximo*, is restless, a demon for perfection, and soon he realizes that the people, his masses, are not yet worthy of themselves. Or of him. Fettered by the inertia of a sluggish history, they are urged to make one supreme effort after another to fulfil their destiny. But what is that destiny, that Utopia? Only the leader knows; he chides, he exhorts, he is restless. He will not let the people rest. Even so, they do, on this Sunday morning, snoozing in purgatory.

But the untutored eye misses much. With every passing hour we will comprehend our surroundings more clearly; first impressions will survive only in the notebook. By the end of the morning we are alert to symbols of activity previously overlooked: for example, the embroidered insignia in almost every street which indicate the local Committees for the Defense of the Revolution. The green trucks parked at street corners are now seen to be filling up with militiamen, and the militiamen look happy. Other trucks, loaded with volunteer work crews, including women and children, roar down the streets in urgent pursuit of their production target (building a hospital, planting coffee, anything). Abruptly we recognize the Revolution.

The Committees for the Defense of the Revolution (CDR) were inspired by the ability of Castro's enemies to explode ten bombs while he was making a public speech in September 1960. He decided, then, to establish block-by-block vigilance committees. But as the years passed and internal security became more secure, the CDR were assigned a wide variety of constructive tasks: helping to cut cane and pick coffee-beans; fighting; loafing; distributing ration cards; encouraging parents to keep their children regularly in school; helping with vaccination campaigns; allocating dwellings, television sets, and children's bicycles; repairing holes in the streets; curbing the black market; and even recouping glass bottles. Now embracing about 4·2 million Cubans out of a total adult population little in excess of five million, and firmly directed by the Cuban Communist Party, the CDR are primarily instruments of ensuring mass participation, physical, mental, and emotional, in the ongoing Revolution. As for the militia, whose mini-skirted girl soldiers once rivalled their Israeli counterparts in the pages of Western picture magazines, its purpose is clearly to provide the maximum defensive capability against armed invasion. A male child may join a brigade at the age of ten, and then serve as a full member from the age of fifteen until he is fifty-five. Armed militiamen are everywhere to be seen guarding public buildings and important installations, in the countryside as well as in the towns. And this is only one respect in which the mood of little Cuba evokes the mood of little Israel—both countries are short of manpower and surrounded by potential aggressors. But, paradoxically, Israel and Cuba are not friends; Israel is aligned to the United States, while Cuba supports the activities of the Palestinian guerrillas.

Footsore, we return for lunch, the first time we have sat down shoulder to shoulder with the fifty or sixty members of our group. Inevitably, meals will involve a certain amount of manoeuvre: three weeks, three meals a day. In such a protracted confrontation with strangers, language factors play their role; the Dutch tend to speak good English but little French, while most of the French adhere to their own tongue. Seated now in the cool dining-room and feeling quite hungry, Martha and I make our separate appraisals round the five tables, estimating compatibility in terms of simple universals: age, expression, dress, couples and singles. (On such tours single travellers must pay extra if they want the luxury of a single room, and even then may have to double up in some provincial stop-overs.)

On my left sits a young man whom we christen the Mad Dutchman. He does not look mad; he looks perfectly normal; and his English, too, is perfect.

'I met a hijacker this morning,' he announces.

'No, really? Where?'

'In a bar.'

'How clever of you. We couldn't find a bar.'

'The bars are disguised as barber shops.'

'Good Lord.'

'Hijacked an Eastern Airlines plane over Baltimore. Regrets it. Nothing to do here.'

'I suppose that is a problem.'

The Mad Dutchman is a marine engineer from Amsterdam. He has visited twenty-eight countries. He speaks six languages fluently. He is thirty-three years old and unmarried.

'Eggs and milk are unobtainable here, you know. For Cubans. Not for us.'

It is not clear to me whether our privileged status causes him pain or pleasure. As with most madmen (or most Dutchmen?), his emotions remain outwardly undifferentiated. He says he intends to hire a bicycle and to meet a lady in Oriente.

Over coffee the Young Swiss lifts his big stomach above the table top and bears down on me. His face, behind the rimless glasses, is a moon of cheese.

26

'Say, you wouldn't happen to have a little ol' Virginia?'
'I beg your pardon?'
'A butt, man,' he says.
I offer him a cigarette and he takes three or four.
'Where did you get that accent?' I ask him.
'I was an American Express vice-president in New York,' he says. 'Crazy, man.'
'I won't hold it against you.'

He blinks and withdraws to chain-smoke the four cigarettes. Next to him, a gnarled tree of a man, with braces supporting his trousers (or suspenders supporting his pants) and a napkin tucked into his check shirt, is eating his lunch as if it were his last. Gobbling, he says nothing, but two intense eyes swivel intelligently in the carved brown features. This is the 'Old Swiss', and we will meet him again.

After lunch we gather in the lounge (where a television set flickers desultorily night and day) and are given details of our itinerary by Nicole and Carlos. We are divided into two groups which will tour the island by different routes to ease the problem of provincial accommodation. Carlos hopes that we will enjoy ourselves and Nicole hopes that we will come to understand the new Cuba. The afternoon, meanwhile, is 'free'. Martha and I groan inwardly and ascend to the first-floor boutique in search of a map of Havana.

But the old French lady with rouged cheeks, Madame Bourgeois, has been there before us. Indeed she has passed the better part of the morning cleaning the place out with thick wads of banknotes; apparently she has many nephews and nieces. Whether or not she has already sent back to France all available maps of Havana, none are to be obtained in the boutique, and the Cuban assistant, without excessive conviction, advises us to try the National Hotel or the Havana Libre. But where are they: in which direction, *por favor*? Would the lady kindly sketch a rough map in my diary, *por favor*? She regards me pityingly: she is not a

cartographer. But the Havana Libre is very tall and generally
—a quick gesture in a windowless room—that way. Her
plump arm flashes towards a pile of toy cowboys stacked
in a corner, miraculously overlooked by Madame Bourgeois.
Silently we descend to the ground floor.

There we come upon the Old Swiss, bent into a kind of
speculative crouch and peering out of the glass doors into the
street in a ferment of massive indecision. I stop beside him
and nod knowingly. But the language locked into this silent
man's head is a mystery.

'We're going for a walk.'

His friendly grin does not indicate comprehension. I lapse
into pidgin French. '*Promener.*'

'*Promenade?*' he says.

'*Ja. Wir spazieren gehen.*' At this he livens up, steps
towards the glass door, steps back again, and stands quiver-
ing with anticipation. 'Map,' I explain. '*Carte. Rien. Stadt-
plan. Nichts.*' Admittedly this, as Martha mutters to me,
isn't very helpful; until you work a few operative verbs into
a language you aren't coming across. The Old Swiss mis-
understands; could he please consult my map of the town?

'No, *nein, noch nicht, am Havana Libre vielleicht.*'

The Old Swiss looks hurt. Clearly I am refusing to show
him my map, a map, moreover, which clearly indicates the
best, quickest, coolest, and sweetest route to the Havana
Libre. My wife intervenes: '*Nous cherchons une carte.*'

Ah! He swivels epileptically, scanning the lobby for our
lost map, and then he gestures as if to say: 'In a country
like this you put down your map to blow your nose, and
the next moment, poof!—gone! Nevertheless, you never
know,' and he begins to amble in searching circles until we
frogmarch him out into the heat. As we plod along the
Malecon, the broad, six-lane highway which runs beside the
sea, the Old Swiss discharges an extraordinary 'Desperanto'
of Swiss German and Swisser French, spliced with guttural

Spanish and, if I am not mistaken, Chinese. The most that I can gather is that he is in a condition of mounting ideological excitement. His noisy progress proves to be of such compelling interest to the whole neighbourhood that my wife's legs mercifully pass unnoticed. There and then I vow to take him everywhere.

Once again the damp heat saps our strength. I look about for a taxi. Havana does still have a few taxis, yellow with black check markings, but they have abandoned the capitalist habit of venturing on to the streets. Instead, they nestle in the shade outside the two or three largest hotels hoping that no one will want a ride. In fact, the streets of Havana are relatively empty of traffic except for the buses and the trucks which carry workers to factories and fields. Apart from the rusting old Buicks, Plymouths, and Chevrolets, one sees the occasional new Renault, Fiat, and Alfa Romeo (several hundred of which, so rumour has it, have been distributed to top officials). Even in the more prosperous Communist countries like the Soviet Union and East Germany, a private car remains for the majority of the population a dream. Even where money is to hand, the waiting-list is forbidding. In Cuba one can simply forget it; a new radio is what you dream about, and perform prodigious feats of voluntary labour to deserve.

As our feet swell and blister, the now-shabby green Leyland buses, imported from Britain (until American pressure put a stop to it), become compellingly attractive. But we are too shy and timid to decipher the bus routes today, although tomorrow we shall do so, discovering that one can travel any distance within the city for five cents, and that buses use separate stops for picking up and putting down their passengers. (Generally the Cuban notion of hospitality does not extend to warning foreigners who are waiting confidently at a put-down stop.)

After a few nervous inquiries we reach the stately National

Hotel, a grandiose memorial to another Cuba. The entrance hall, regally structured, its ceilings spun from beautiful Cuban woods, its leather sofas deep and confident, is humming with Soviet technicians and their suntanned families, who live permanently in the hotel. The Old Swiss collapses into a chair, overwhelmed by so much opulence, and I begin my search for a map of Havana. But there is none. Some are expected shortly, but shortly can mean any time. Do these favoured Russians possess maps? Of course they do. Their pockets are heavy with maps, their stout wives are fanning themselves with maps, their children are wearing paper hats folded out of maps. We are automatically directed to the great Havana Libre and find ourselves once again out in the grey heat, very thirsty and close to tears, dreaming nostalgically of those despicable profiteers who overcharge you for a cold drink or an ice-cream at a street corner in the decadent West.

Sunstroke has reinforced the Old Swiss's loquacity. I abandon the attempt to understand him until, spying the tall Havana Libre Hotel, he cries 'Hilton' with a hideous cackle and twists his strong hands in a gesture of strangulation. I gather, now, that this garage mechanic from near Zurich is politically somewhere to the Left of Mao Tsetung. Formerly the Havana Hilton, the transformed Havana Libre stands as a symbol of the new order, purged of its brash, vulgar, perfumed, hustling, *nouveaux riches*, available to the common people at modest prices, and generally serving as a gigantic hold-all for out-of-town peasant delegations, conferences, planning committees, and foreign students. It is incredibly ugly. The interior reminds me of a railway station during a strike. Two inherited signs announce, in English, 'Coffee Shop' and 'Cafeteria'. Hope sparks in us. We enter the cafeteria, which is clearly func tioning but almost empty. Enticing urns of cold orange, lemon, and pineapple drink gleam on the counter. Salvation!

Crazed by thirst, we stumble towards them. A waiter approaches us to ask whether we are residents of the hotel. No use in cheating; he would want to see proof. I protest, implore. The *señora* is dying. He is adamant. Let her die. In the coffee shop it is the same story.

We enter an office which announces itself as a tourist bureau. We are politely ejected and directed vaguely towards another office which apparently handles foreigners dying of thirst. We find it. It is open. A staff of five young men and women are sitting about chatting gaily, surrounded by pretty travel posters and empty desks. One of the girls speaks French. We are looking for a map of the city, *s'il vous plaît*.

'A map of Havana?'

'Yes.'

'A street map or a map of the bus routes?'

'Both, if possible.'

Now, I ask you: imagine yourself entering a shop and demanding film for your camera. The assistant immediately responds, 'Black-and-white or colour?' Would not such a reaction indicate to you that the shop does indeed stock film? And would you not be surprised if he then told you that he carried no film at all? But such, indeed, is our luck at the Havana Libre. The staff of five are nothing if not helpful. Maps, they explain, are in great demand, particularly among foreigners dying of thirst. The relevant Government printing office has promised a new supply of maps which are expected to arrive 'shortly'. Meanwhile we should try the National Hotel. We have? Then try the Hotel Deauville. It's quite a long walk and they advise us to take a bus.

At least we have salvaged something from this expedition: we know which bus to take. But first we snatch a seat in the hotel lobby and I reflect a little on the old Cuba which the Havana Hilton once symbolized and which passed away more than ten years ago. In those days public office benefited the holder. The distribution of jobs, the manipulation of Government contracts, and the gerrymandering of economic regulations ensured that. Nepotism was the rule. The number of 'officials' was enormous—a hundred and eighty-five thousand, or eleven per cent of the employed population. And most of these officials from the highest to the lowest were the pawns of politicians. The politicians were drawn almost exclusively from the middle and upper classes (the wealthiest of whom married into North American families) whose prosperity was derived from real estate, tax evasion, usury, and corruption, from sinecures and lottery transactions. Unproductive and shallow in their sense of Cuban identity, this parasitical class affected American ways and adopted English names for their 'yacht clubs' and 'country clubs'. (Membership of the Havana Biltmore Yacht Club, for example, was dependent on a three-thousand-dollar shareholding in it.) As for politics, they accepted despotism and gangsterism as the norm, so long as it protected their wealth. About one hundred thousand businessmen, bankers, and administrators committed themselves irrevocably to the Batista régime. When Castro suddenly took power some of the big companies panicked and splashed out newspaper advertisements to congratulate the new Government. As a gesture of solidarity, the Telephone Company even paid its taxes in advance! But to no avail.

Reaching the Hotel Deauville, we bid adieu to the Old Swiss and take a dip in the sixth-floor swimming-pool. My accumulated aches and grievances ebb gently into the warm water. We have flogged ourselves, but to some purpose. Only the snail-like pedestrian can properly assimilate the sounds, smells, rhythms, moods, and kaleidoscopic images of the strange city, grasping its essential dignity, the implicit self-confidence of its people, its claim to a place in history. It may be a city without maps, but I already discern that it belongs to Cubans. Drying in the sun, I gaze down to the sea where a dredger is patiently removing silt from the harbour entrance (the Soviet oil-tankers have deep hulls), and then, lo and behold, into view comes such a tanker, flying both the red Soviet flag and the blue-and-white Cuban one, the umbilical cord of a country still in a state of foetus-like dependence. A scattering of small fishing boats hovers on the horizon. Beyond that horizon, to the north, lies the United States of America. Turning, I let my eye wander over the patched roof-tops to the old Presidential Palace with its triumphant pinnacles of marzipan.

We collapse onto our twin beds and Martha immediately sinks into a brief Churchillian sleep from which she will presently surface bright-eyed and ready for anything. I drag myself to my notebook and scribble down my impressions before they are overlayed by others. This done, I pick up the Spanish phrase-book and flick through it despondently, aware that the only way to learn a language is to learn it properly, two hours a day for two years, and without fail. An hour later Martha comes out of the bathroom to announce that the lavatory cistern is not all that it might be; at which I display an unsuspected mastery of hydraulic engineering—and will continue to do so, the length and breadth of Cuba, wherever the level of water pressure does not stymie me completely.

Cocktail time. The bar is in the basement and dimly lit. Most Cuban hotels have a flourishing bar (for residents only) with an Afro-Cuban band to drown conversation and drinks at varying prices to keep you guessing. Apart from beer, rum is the basis of everything you can afford; imported drinks like whisky, gin, and even vodka are prohibitively expensive. My wife soon displays an ominous addiction to Daiquiris, so frothy and feminine in their snow-crushed ice, and so quickly absorbed at forty cents a time. The whirr of the electric mixer, I notice, sends her into an almost erotic trance. Growing cunning with time, I learn to place a glass of iced water beside her first Daiquiri, a miserly gesture which binds her to the barman in mutual disdain. The barmen in the Deauville are old hands, oiled and dapper, and I occasionally wonder why they did not take off for Miami years ago—perhaps Miami is overloaded with barmen. I try a Havana Club Dry cocktail but am a dollar the poorer, and will henceforward oscillate between beer and the enticing variety of gaily coloured drinks which bear charming names but little serious alcohol. At mid-day I am always game for a Cuba Libre, a sweetened fruit drink which is relatively cheap.

Our guide Carlos diffidently joins us at the bar. On a long trip it is important to win the confidence of the guide, to peel away his official reserve, his official optimism, his official explanations. There is no formula for doing this, but in the case of Carlos I guess that my age and sex may help. And tact, too. A Communist guide (and not only a Communist guide) will probably show you the cold shoulder if, initially, you criticize everything you see and draw invidious comparisons. He does not demand that you be a Communist, a socialist, or anything, but he needs to feel in you a fundamental goodwill towards his country, a sense of curiosity, and the desire to learn. A Cuban guide is on his guard not so much against bourgeois prejudices or a faith in private enterprise (he may enjoy an argument), as against that innate superiority complex which Europeans and Americans tend to carry in their baggage when they visit less economically developed countries. And there are other elementary rules of tact to be observed. Don't make persistent claims on his attention, don't try to monopolize his time, don't always sit next to him at table or in the coach. He has the other passengers to consider and to be seen to consider. Above all, bear in mind that a night's indiscretion does not make an affair; when the morning comes, reassure him with the slightest gesture that he need regret nothing he has said.

Carlos tells us about his visits to the Soviet Union and

China. He enjoyed the Russian trip very much, but China was marred by his inability to cope with chopsticks and by what he calls Chinese 'racism'. On one occasion he visited a remote Chinese village where black people had been neither seen nor heard of. A crowd of children gathered to stare at him and giggle. After much nudging and debate, one of the boldest, a small girl, tentatively approached him, paused to assess his friendliness, and then, reassured, began to rub the back of his hand with her finger. Nothing came off on her finger. Licking it, she tried again, but the black paint was stubborn.

'That doesn't sound such a terrible story,' I suggest.

But Carlos is adamant. The Chinese are racists; the Chinese believe they are superior to everyone else; never once during his visit to China did anyone display the slightest curiosity about Cuba. 'Listen, David, the Russians are not racists but the Chinese ... I would not want to go back there.'

'Is racial prejudice in Cuba so completely a thing of the past?'

'Yes, of course. The Revolution put an end to it.'

'Can such ingrained prejudices be eradicated so abruptly?'

'Fidel has made it clear that racism has no place in our society.'

This, of course, is the kind of answer you get during a first conversation. Two weeks hence, Carlos will speak more flexibly on the subject of Cuban race-relations. Meanwhile, there will be ample opportunity to harvest one's own impressions.

The Negroes were brought to Cuba in chains by the Spaniards early in the sixteenth century. Although the slave-trade was officially abolished in 1820, Negroes continued to be illegally imported as slaves for a further fifty years. Early in the present century the black population was reinforced by immigrants from Jamaica and Haiti looking for employment. But blacks and mulattos still comprise less than one-third of the total population. About half of them live in Oriente, the poorest of Cuba's six provinces. In addition, there are a considerable number of *mestizos*, people of racially mixed parentage, Negro-Chinese or white-Chinese. (In certain other parts of Latin America *mestizo* denotes an Indian-Spanish mixture, but, although there were an estimated two hundred thousand Indians living in Cuba at the time of Columbus's arrival, they were subsequently exterminated and left no survivors.) The Chinese element is mainly descended from about one hundred and fifty thousand labourers imported from China during the third quarter of the nineteenth century to supplement the slave work-force.

Admittedly, Cuba never had Jim Crow laws. There was, in fact, some formal intermarriage. But even after slavery faded out in the 1870s, the blacks tended to be worse paid and worse educated than the white creoles. (A *criollo* is a white person, usually of Spanish origin, who was born in Cuba or who settled in Cuba and identified with the Cuban nationality and outlook. In British terms, pre-1776 Americans would be creoles.) Before 1959 Negroes were barred from the posher hotels and from the private beaches patronized by Americans and by upper-crust Cubans. In some cities, public squares had a promenade reserved for whites, a step higher than the one allowed to blacks.

Many poor blacks served in Batista's army and police-force. Most of them were not impressed by Castro before he came to power, regarding him as merely another upper-class Castilian pushing for power and privilege. But Castro's assault on discrimination quickly won black sentiment to the Revolutionary programme. A survey made by the American sociologist Maurice Zeitlin in the summer of 1962 indicated that whereas support for the Revolution was only sixty-seven per cent among white proletarians, it ran as high as eighty per cent among black workers.

Today there is not a trace or a shadow of formal racial discrimination in Cuba. Castro himself has loudly supported the Black Power movement in the United States and warmly welcomed militants like Stokely Carmichael to Havana (although others, notably Elridge Cleaver, have later denounced what they regard as Castro's inadequate support for black revolutionary programmes). In the second Declaration of Havana (1962), he said, 'Latin America's fifteen million Negroes and fourteen million mulattos know to their horror and anger that their brothers to the north cannot ride the same buses as their white compatriots, or even die in the same hospitals.' The black Cuban poet Nicolás Guillén expresses such feelings violently in his 'How to Become a Southern Governor':

> When you have taught your dog
> to pounce upon a Negro
> and rip his guts for a snack
>
> when you have learned
> how to bark
> and wag your tail,
>
> Then be happy,
> WHITE MAN,
>
> You can be Governor
> of your state.*

And yet ... In 1965, only one member out of ten of the Cuban Communist Party's Central Committee had black blood. In the same year the black Cuban Communist Carlos Moore denounced the Castro régime in the magazine *Présence Africaine* as yet another example of camouflaged white supremacism. Such a judgment is certainly excessive.

* Translated by Lenox and Maryanne Raphael.

The head of the Cuban armed forces, subordinate only to the Castro brothers, is a black, Comandante Juan Almeida, and even if one explains away this appointment as 'liberal tokenism', it remains a fact that liberal tokenism has not yet carried a black into the American Joint Chiefs of Staff.

What one does observe is that the citizens of Havana still tend to move about in 'shade groups'. Couples strolling in the street, couples queuing for an ice-cream, couples sitting in the cinema, are almost invariably of the same race. The key to this inherent ghetto restraint, this binding web of historically received preferences, is sexual. When men gather at street corners to pass the time of day and to girl-watch, they mingle easily with black and white companions. But where the relations of men and women are involved, it is another, older, family-inhibited story. As for the black woman of Havana, she still applies to her hair hot irons, dyes, and scissors in emulation of the white woman.

In Cuba one sees neither Afro hair-cuts nor Afro clothes. I doubt whether this should occasion surprise. The American Afro style has, after all, very little to do with the physical or national aspirations of contemporary Africans, but is, rather, an essentially extravagant and 'primitivist' gesture of dissociation in a society where all public gestures from Madison Avenue commercials to East Village protests achieve an impact only when extravagant, and where, moreover, the promise of genuine integration has rung too hollow for too long. One notices, also, that 'busy' societies of modest means and limited leisure are not responsive to politics-as-aesthetics, which they distrust as a symptom of super-affluent individualism. (In 1968, the Czechoslovak students, beavering for a greater measure of democracy, were nonplussed by the flamboyant anarchism of the Parisian rebels.) An Afro hair-cut on a man would most probably strike most Cuban blacks as both effeminate and a retrogression from bi-racial national solidarity. One hears rumours of violent outbursts of Caribbean voodoo and black magic, but that, of course, belongs to a different scene.

At dinner the Old Swiss waves to us from another table. It is clear that he has not changed his shirt since leaving Zurich. The Mad Dutchman is nowhere to be seen and I can only assume he has hijacked a bicycle or been hijacked by one. (We will not see him again for three weeks; he has been assigned to the other group.) Madame Bourgeois is reminiscing about riding an elephant in India, and how she only wished she could have carried its tusks home as gifts for her nephews and nieces. She owns fourteen apartments in Paris and is most cheerful about the rents they bring in. Nicole announces the forthcoming expropriation of all Parisian landlords and *rentiers*, but Madame Bourgeois has heard that before and advises Nicole, not without malice, to marry a rich young man. Monsieur Lepinay, a senior technician from Saint-Etienne, and a member of the French Communist Party, is discoursing on the subject of economic infrastructures and contradictions within the market economy. The Young Swiss, parking himself beside me, begins to smoke my cigarettes and to discharge hideously pseudo-colloquial Americanisms which run out of steam in mid-sentence. His 'vibes are bad, man'; Cuba is 'a big deal like hell'; almost everything I say to him is 'right on'; he regrets the passing of the brothels which, so he hears, were 'real cool'. I gather from his disjointed polyglotese that he has come to Cuba to confirm his faith in free enterprise and American Express and that a single day has been enough to show him all he needs to see of a country where the populace must queue up for everything. Wolfing his food, he offers as his own a definition of socialism I have heard before: 'nothing, evenly divided'.

Castro knows what the Young Swiss is saying. Back in April 1962, speaking in Matanzas, Castro said: 'This is a revolution which must be ashamed of itself because it is forced to ration *malanga*. And the imperialists are saying to Latin Americans: "There is your socialism: hunger, shortages, rationing..."' At that time beans and potatoes were unavailable, and there was a shortage of meat, chickens, fish, eggs, and milk. But shame does not rescue an economy; since 1962 rationing has remained in force, imposed both by the loss of American imports and by a decline in production at home. By 1965 agricultural production per head had fallen to seventy per cent of the pre-1959 level. At the same time, Cuba must export a high proportion of its foodstuffs in a vain attempt to reduce its mounting debt to the Communist states of Eastern Europe. Long lines form outside the food shops. Although no one goes hungry, only the most cunning or the most patient collect their due after a huge waste of time and energy. The black market begins with the private-sector peasants—where there is rationing there is always a black market, however stringent the penalties.

Clothes, too, are rationed. Each citizen is entitled to so many shoes per year. Scarcity was most acute in 1968-69, but subsequently there has been some improvement. Fuel-rationing was announced at the turn of 1967-68. When our coach refills its tanks I note that ten gallons costs only three pesos, but such prices are deceptive in so far as Soviet oil reaches the consumer at a subsidized rate, and the supply is restricted by a quota system rather than by market forces. Nevertheless, when commodities are in short supply, a system of allocation is more equitable than an inflationary spiral which benefits only the rich.

A new day dawns. At this equatorial latitude, day and night share the clock in roughly equal proportions throughout the year, just as the average temperature in summer is only minimally higher than in winter. Such monotony, such climatic perseverance would, I think, eventually drive me round the bend. In England a December night begins at four-thirty p.m., a June night at nine-thirty, and I like it that way just as I need the clearly defined mood of the four seasons, the ebb and flow of nature, the dramatic rhythm of the year. From such sources humans derive their energies, their renewed hopes, their cunning, their techniques of conservation. A lethargic climate interspersed by violent hurricanes or tornadoes breeds an apathetic people who periodically thin their ranks by mutual massacre. And yet such notions do not really persuade me, they reflect too faithfully that cranky, self-serving geo-politics which dominated Germanic theories of racial superiority from the time of Bismarck to the time of Hitler.

After breakfast we begin, appropriately, at the beginning —with sixteenth-century Havana. Our two cheerful coach-drivers, the short, dark Pedro and the older, more urbane Rafael (a great hooter of his horn at ladies in the street), set our Soviet engine into noisy animation and transport us down a maze of narrow, one-way streets. But our first port of call comes all too soon; congenitally lazy, once comfortably seated in a bus I abhor the effort of dismounting.

On the edge of the sea, perched on a promontory and guarding the harbour entrance, stand the fortress of La Punta and the Morro Castle. Cuba boasts several ancient coastal forts, including El Morro of Santiago de Cuba (henceforward referred to simply as Santiago, not to be confused with the capital of Chile), El Morrillo, and the Castillo de San Severino—both at Matanzas, and the Jagua Castle at Cienfuegos. El Morro, Havana, which dates from 1587-97, was built under the stimulus of the unwelcome appearance of Sir Francis Drake in 1585. La Punta, likewise built in the sixteenth century, is now at the disposal of the small Cuban Navy.

A few hundred yards away, further up the channel leading to the main harbour, stands the Castillo de la Fuerza, protected by massive walls and a deep moat. Started in 1558, with the purpose of protecting the city from corsairs and pirates, it is said to be the oldest building in Cuba and one of the oldest forts in the world (but guides are somewhat unreliable about such claims). A tower built in 1632 supports a weather-vane representing a beautiful girl, romantically called La Giraldilla—and indeed the city of La Habana itself is named after the first Indian girl to have greeted the incoming Spaniards, a gesture of hospitality her people certainly lived to regret. La Fuerza still carries in white marble the coat of arms of the house of Hapsburg, which, at the peak of its power in the time of the Emperor Charles V, reigned supreme over both the Holy Roman Empire and the Spanish dominions.

Carlos dutifully explains these things, but in a listless manner occasionally livened by sarcasm. For him, evidently, the past was a compound of evil and folly, of tyrants and slave-traders, of false gods and superstition. For the descendant of slaves such a perspective is perhaps inescapable. For myself, I am much attached to the past, warts and all, feeling myself to be inextricably bound to it, and although I do not subscribe to the image of Francis Drake conveyed in television serials, the dashing Protestant avenger of flashing eye and gleaming sword, I do indeed view him as an authentic moment in the European adventure. Cruel, yes; rapacious, yes; exploitative, yes—but, nevertheless, one of those Renaissance captains who fashioned their own frontiers and gave their blind eye to God. But Carlos hears only the rattle of chains.

Let us squat down in the shade, lean our backs against the ramparts, and sign on for the briefest of history lessons. Cuba was discovered (or, if you care about the Indians, 'discovered') by Columbus in 1492 and conquered for Spain by Diego Velásquez in 1511. Spain held on to Cuba for almost four hundred years, until long after her other New World colonies were lost to her. Velásquez founded Havana. Fifteen years later the first slaves were imported from Africa. Sugar became an important commodity during the last decade of the sixteenth century. When the British took Jamaica in 1655, a number of Spanish settlers fled to Cuba. Coffee was first planted in 1748. In 1762 Lord Albemarle turned up to claim Cuba for Britain, for George III, and he had sufficient force at his disposal to make his point. However, the British quickly traded off the island in exchange for Florida, which, of course, was eventually subverted from within by disloyal elements calling themselves Americans. In the nineteenth century, affected by the twin examples of the American and French Revolutions, independence movements arose throughout Latin America, and Cuba was no exception. A Negro rising was savagely suppressed in 1837. In 1851 various leaders of the Cuban independence movement were shot, but another ten-year war began in 1868, and the Cuban nationalists known as *mambises*, who fought in these wars, are highly celebrated in Castro's Cuba as precursors of the small band of freedom fighters who landed from the little ship *Granma* on the coast of Oriente in December 1956. But of all these nineteenth-century heroes, by far the most sanctified is José Martí, whose white-plaster bust stands on a pedestal in almost every town square and outside almost every school in Cuba.

Martí (1853-95) was a brilliant Cuban intellectual of Spanish parentage. When still at school his imagination and patriotism were fired by the outbreak of civil war in 1868. Having founded a newspaper and published romantic writings on behalf of the rebels, he was imprisoned. Pardoned and released, but forced to live abroad, he studied law at Madrid and Saragossa. In 1878 he returned to Cuba under a general amnesty but, finding a climate of stagnation and despondency, moved to New York where he lived for ten years. (It was Martí who introduced Walt Whitman to

Spanish-American readers.) An agnostic, a freemason, and a devoted disciple of Emerson and Longfellow, he nevertheless expounded anti-American sentiments which Fidel Castro is not reluctant to quote. As when, for example, he wrote in May 1895 of the need to prevent by force of arms the 'annexation of all the nations of our America by the violent and brutal North which despises us ...' Determined to prove his physical courage, this frail intellectual landed a small rebel force at Playitas, demanding full independence for Cuba and not mere autonomy. On 19 May 1895 he was killed in a skirmish, three years before the North American 'Monster' in whose 'lair' he had lived made the move he had anticipated and feared. When the USS *Maine* blew up in Havana harbour in 1898, the United States readily seized on the pretext for war, blockaded Havana, and defeated the Spanish fleet at Santiago. Cuba gained her 'independence' and the US gained a colony. We shall return to this theme later.

We mount the bus and take a slow journey through the charming old Plaza das Armas, which is dominated by the Cathedral of San Cristóbal, the patron saint of Havana. The Cathedral was founded by the Jesuits in 1704, but the Jesuits have long since surrendered to other caretakers, who make it impossible—as we discovered on two subsequent independent visits—to get inside. As repetition induces familiarity, the basic style of colonial Spanish architecture becomes clear to me: houses are built in the shape of a square round a central *patio* which is open to the sky and usually graced by old palm trees rising above the level of the roof.

The National History Museum, once the residence of Cuba's Spanish Governors, is built in this style. It is already night when we arrive there, and a large audience is seated in the *patio* on canvas chairs, enraptured by a melancholy singer. As we file across their line of vision they regard us with a gay and sympathetic curiosity. Upstairs, we are shown a splendid collection of uniforms worn by Spanish officers, others worn by creole regiments loyal to Spain, and still others, far simpler, worn by rebel nationalists. Standards, flags, and medals abound in the midst of drawing-room interiors, stylized portraits, and examples of the thick, black garments worn during all those years of tropical heat by the respectable Cuban bourgeoisie. In a glass case one comes upon a letter from the King of Spain and another, dated 1902, from Theodore Roosevelt, ending the American military occupation, granting Cuba 'self-government' but carefully saying nothing about real independence. Turning, one is confronted by an armoury of machetes and crossbows used with terrible effect—so Carlos explains—by the rough and rude peasants who shed their blood for an independent Cuba. The rebel general who perfected the machete as a weapon of war, and is thereby held in awesome regard, Máximo Gómez, glowers at us from the wall with eyes so fierce that I break into laughter and have to retire into a corner, disgraced.

CHAPTER

2

More of Havana

I should explain one thing. We are travelling as members of a group-tour because the only way to visit Cuba is as a member of a delegation or a tourist party, unless one has a job lined up, as a properly accredited journalist, or a spy. Most Communist states regard the individual tourist as both an uneconomical proposition and an administrative nuisance. They prefer, characteristically, centralization and planning. The Cuban Institute of Friendship with the Peoples, supported by a generous budget, accords hospitality to official visitors and delegations. The Cuban Tourist Commission (INIT) takes care of the rest—us. Like the Soviet Intourist, it controls all the hotels open to foreigners, fixes the tariff for meals and accommodation, deploys its own fleet of coaches, employs the guides, negotiates with foreign tourist agencies, and generally adopts a bureaucratic approach to happiness. The lone-wolf breed of traveller will certainly find the restrictions irksome, but he has to concede that he is being offered extraordinarily good value for his money.

Let me give two illustrations of this. The previous year, in the fall of 1971, we embarked on a similar tour of the Soviet Union. First, consider the distances we travelled by air: from London to Moscow, from Moscow to Irkutsk in eastern Siberia, from Irkutsk westwards to Novosibirsk, then south into Asia Minor, taking in Alma Ata, Tashkent, Bukhara, and Samarkand, before heading back to Moscow and thence to London. A total span of ten or eleven thousand miles. In the course of our journey we stayed in seven hotels and ate, I suppose, more than forty sound, if not always exciting, meals. We enjoyed the services of both a general guide and of local guides and were only very occasionally charged extra for a special coach excursion. The total cost of this holiday was a mere five hundred dollars (each).

And so to Cuba. The round-trip from Prague to Havana is nine or ten thousand miles. In the course of slightly over three weeks we stay in ten hotels, drive the length and breadth of the island, eat more than sixty meals, enjoy a brief taste of luxury, and return home only eight hundred dollars the poorer (each).

It goes without saying that neither Intourist nor the Cuban Institución Nacional de la Industria Turistica is attempting to make a fat profit out of tourism. Certainly they need the hard foreign currency in which they are paid, and certainly they do not weep when the thirsty or acquisitive tourist begins to cash traveller's cheques in dollars, pounds, or francs. But for them tourism is primarily a weapon of propaganda. They believe they have something admirable to show and they want to show it. Does this mean that they allow the foreigner to see only 'showplaces' especially erected for his benefit, sweeping the dust and dirt under the carpet? Is he therefore doomed to be hoodwinked? It is interesting how many visitors to Communist countries are so convinced of this that they never stop shouting 'they can't fool me', view everything through tightly blinkered preconceptions, force themselves to disparage an excellent ballet, play, or opera with remarks like 'yes, but who can afford this kind of thing?—only the upper crust, I bet', and generally clutch their breasts against the danger of political rape. Such people come out little wiser than they went in. In truth, exposure to an alien social system need be less menacing than is often supposed. Beliefs, prejudices, and values instilled during the course of twenty, thirty, sixty years are not to be unravelled and shredded in the course of two or three weeks. Both the Russians and the Cubans are generous—sometimes too generous—with free time, which allows the tourist to wander at will through a city, observing, probing, judging. Although the tour is 'conducted', ultimately the symphony emerges from the soil, the streets, the angle of shoulder blades, the shop windows, the air itself. If you return home a 'duped fellow-traveller', you have only yourself to blame.

The things that the Russians or the Cubans want the foreigner to see genuinely reflect social priorities. Both in the West and in the Communist countries historical buildings, monuments, zoos, theatres, galleries, museums, beauty spots, and pleasure resorts are regarded as part and parcel of tourism; but whereas the tourist in the West tends to spend his spare time and money in restaurants, bars, nightclubs, and cinemas, in Russia or Cuba he is despatched in pursuit of factories, farms, schools, universities, housing projects, and research institutes. In other words, his holiday is not treated as an escape from the mundane productive world of toil, but as a chance to penetrate the virtues of its socialist model. But here a small irony intrudes. Did you ever visit a cement factory in your own country, or a school for young fishermen, or an automobile plant? If not, a socialist one will be your first. You may return home an expert on the cultivation of pineapples, cotton, or sugar, while knowing nothing of the techniques employed by the corn farmers of Iowa or the wine-growers of Burgundy. Such is the division

49

of labour in the affluent West that the white- and blue-collar spheres of work remain mutual mysteries.

The Parque Central accommodates both the National Theatre and the Capitol, a vulgar and pretentious imitation of the Washington Capitol, opened in 1929 to house the Cuban legislature. It is now a science museum and exhibition centre. (Castro's Cuba lacks even a sham legislature.)

'You don't have any elected representatives in your country?' I ask Carlos.

'The will of the people is heard at all levels.'

We enter the Capitol and embark on one of those rituals of respect for the cultural deities which account for the shuffling feet and glazed eyes of tourists the world over. We are greeted by 'Primitive Man And His Family', local model; he resembles other models, and we meander past him into an ambitious mock-up of a grotto on the Isle of Pines once inhabited by Indians. The walls are decorated with paintings whose mosaic daubs of red and blue bring to mind the work of Dubuffet.

'These grottoes are now inhabited by political prisoners, of course,' I say to Martha loudly enough for Nicole to hear. The bait is taken.

'Cuba has no political prisoners,' Nicole says sharply. 'Terrorists, spies, and counter-revolutionaries are not political prisoners, merely criminals.'

'Really? When Castro himself was imprisoned after Moncado, was he a terrorist, a mere criminal, or a political prisoner?'

'All such parallels are false. Fidel was fighting for the liberation of the Cuban people.'

A museum guide, a poker-faced lady whose demeanour is one of standardized solemnity, hushes our chatter and conducts us along a row of illuminated models which depict the evolution of Cuban sugar production from the days of slavery to the era of American domination. Carlos translates for poker-face, whose set-speech he must have heard all too often. Already I am beginning to daydream; it's a disgraceful habit.

'It was in this building that the corrupt representatives of the bourgeoisie ...'

Carlos is taking the opportunity to expose the Capitol as a sham-tribute to so-called American democracy. And so we are back, for the moment, with Cuban history. The United States declared war on Spain in April 1898. On 10 December the Treaty of Paris was signed, whereby Spain renounced all sovereignty over Cuba. (Significantly, the Cubans themselves were not even represented at the conference.) General Leonard Wood, stern and incorruptible, was appointed Military Governor. On 2 March 1901 the notorious Platt Amendment was attached by Congress to the Army Appropriation Bill for 1901-2. Besides demanding the exclusive use of certain Cuban coaling and naval stations like Guantánamo for a derisory rent, the Amendment insisted on the United States's right to intervene 'for the preservation of Cuban independence, the maintenance of a government adequate for the protection of life, property, and individual liberty ...' (One might call this, adapting Rousseau's phrase, forcing your neighbour to be free.)

Within the next twenty-five years at least five attempted revolutions were thwarted by the intervention or threatened intervention of US Marines. American troops landed in Cuba in 1906, 1912, and 1920.

Most Cuban Governments were corrupt or worse, but the presidency of Gerardo Machado (1924-33) was marked by a particularly revolting tyranny. In August 1933 he was ousted by a military coup, and from the ranks of the insurgent army the obscure Sergeant Fulgencio Batista emerged, to become President from 1940 to 1944. At the end of his term he retired to his Florida estate. His successors,

137140

Ramón Grau San Martín and Carlos Prío Socarras, were members of the Cuban Revolutionary Party, known as the Autentico, and, as such, committed to democratic reform. But their compromises did not please the purists, who broke away in 1946 to form the rival Ortodoxo party. Every aspiring political faction promised to put a stop to the corruption, nepotism, violence, and general gangsterism which dominated political life, but, once in power, found these strategies indispensable to their own survival. It was as an Ortodoxo candidate that the young Fidel Castro ran for Congress in 1952; had he been elected, one thing is certain : the history of modern Cuba would have been very different. But the election never took place. Tiring of his comfortable exile, Batista staged a coup in March 1952 and Cuba entered another period of outright dictatorship.

But we have not yet completed our tour of the Capitol. My friend the Old Swiss, still wearing the same shirt, is cavorting excitedly in front of a glass case full of stuffed snakes, scorpions, sharks, sword-fish, and spiders, no doubt trapped by the nightmares of a childhood from which, forty years later, his stern Swiss parents will not allow him to escape. Carlos taps me on the shoulder and beckons me to come and see 'the real thing', while Nicole, quickening her step, announces 'la salle impérialiste'.

'La salle impérialiste' turns out to be the Vietnam room. This is our first encounter with the Cuban obsession with Vietnam. In the centre of a large hall of shame the remnants of a shot-down US fighter-bomber have been lovingly pieced together, along with the pilot's survival kit, maps, plastic folders of gold coins, and a sheet of injunctions, printed in several Asiatic languages, to treat him as a friend or, failing that, according to the rules of the Geneva Convention. The display lacks, in fact, only the mummified pilot. Apart from photographs illustrating Cuban–Vietnamese solidarity, including one of Fidel caressing a prize Vietnamese bull (Fidel towers over the diminutive Hanoi leaders but not over the bull), there is also a display of primitive weapons and spiked traps devised by Vietcong guerrillas or, as the Cubans put it, by the Vietnamese people. I had better admit that I am in complete sympathy with all this. At the time of our visit the US Air Force is bombing the dikes, and the approaches to Haiphong have been mined.

Seven years previously, in 1965, two friends and I had pulled off something of a coup, organizing the Oxford Teach-In on Vietnam at only five days' notice, attracting full television and live radio coverage, the presence of the British Foreign Secretary and, in view of that, precipitating a special journey by President Johnson's spokesman, Henry Cabot Lodge. It was my duty to look after our American guest, and I shall never forget his grim and angry expression after he had delivered a thirty-minute speech which aroused in one section of his undergraduate audience a spirit of audible derision. Not, I must stress, that he was shouted down, pelted with eggs, or driven from the platform; these were pre-New Left days and his reception was well within the code of conduct traditionally accepted by the Oxford Union (the Debating Society) where the Teach-In was held. 'I would never have come,' Mr Cabot Lodge growled to me afterwards, 'if I had known that this great university had become a hotbed of Communism.'

It was not, of course, a remark for public release. But it amply reflected that paranoiac and Manichean view of world politics which had cast a pall of fear and inhibition over American life in the 1950s. (The Russians have shared this view with equal conviction, merely turning its basic assumptions inside out.) Both Presidents Johnson and Nixon have revealed a psychological incapacity to distinguish opposition from treason, and both have evidently believed that a good cause (napalming the Vietnamese) justifies any number of lies, evasions, and covert acts of intimidation. The White

53

House has, in effect, become a permanent, one-man police riot, with the trigger-happy sheriff surrounded by private retainers whose main task is to blackmail, bludgeon, wire-tap, burgle, and tax-trap his critics.

Perhaps the French majority of our party are thinking along these lines, I don't know, but one thing is clear, *la salle impérialiste* has provoked them to a unanimous out-burst of anti-American feeling. They seem to be competing to prove to Cuba their virtue, to cash in their credentials, aware as they must be that France herself, supported by a generous American subsidy, had done all in her power to suppress Ho Chi Minh until, in 1954, she was forced to give up the fight. Inspired by this atmosphere, Nicole launches into a clinical exposition of how American planes and gun-ships are shot down, and of how—she throws me a chal-lenging glance—successive British Governments, including the one led by the '*soi-disant travailliste Vill-sohn*' ('the so-called Labourite Wilson'), have failed to condemn American genocide in Vietnam. She pauses here, offering me the chance to put my neck in the noose. I say nothing. She is perfectly correct, and besides, these are early days. But Madame Lepinay, the tiny wife of the Communist technician from Saint-Etienne, a lady who does not speak often, is not satis-fied with my silence. For her, America begins just across La Manche, the English Channel, and she has tasted blood.

'What do you say, Monsieur l'Anglais?'

There is, of course, an effective rhetorical answer: Madame, I do not hold *you* personally responsible for the Algerian war, therefore ... But heat is not light and I merely confess that Nicole is quite right.

Everyone looks rather disappointed, particularly Nicole who no doubt still remembers my somewhat truculent reaction to the confiscation of our books at the airport.

On this note we move from the war room to the peace room, where we find imported models of Soviet lunar craft

trundling about the surface of the moon. Carlos delivers a
short lecture on the exploration of space and Martha looks
bored, not so much by space as by the familiarity of the
lecture. It was bigger and better in Moscow.

As the others drift out of the room I remark to Carlos:

'I suppose the *Yanquis* have jumped six inches off the
ground?'

Carlos looks puzzled. 'Please?' He bends towards me
politely.

'Sent men to the moon,' I explain.

He grins and flicks sweat off his brow in a gesture
peculiarly his own. 'So we hear,' he says, disarming me.
Nicole, however, now perpetually poised to cope with out-
breaks of delinquency on my part, explains that if we wish
to learn about American space exploration we should go
to the United States.

'Is that a very scientific attitude?'

'Cuba is able to display Soviet lunar craft due to her frater-
nal relations with the Soviet Academy of Science. Cuba
enjoys no such co-operation from the Americans.'

'Quite so. I was merely questioning a lecture which made
no mention of American successes in space.'

'I am sure you know all about those already,' says Nicole
drily.

'When we were in Moscow last year,' Martha says, 'we
visited the Soviet space exhibition and found photographs
of the American astronauts. That seems a sensible attitude.'

Martha has the last word and Carlos does not mind at all.
As we leave the Capitol I ask him whether he plays chess.

'Of course. And you? You want a game?'

'Thank you. But I'm sure you're better than I am. Cuba
has a great chess tradition, I mean Capablanca and ...'

'I am not Capablanca,' Carlos says. He waves me up the
steps into the coach. 'Who are you supporting in Iceland?'
he asks.

'Spassky. And you?'

He shrugs. 'This Feescher is a strange man. But a good chess player. He is very fond of money, yes?'

'Yes, very.'

Carlos smiles and turns away. I like this man. He is a true son of the Cuban Revolution—open, honest, relaxed, and confident. He is also the son of illiterate peasants, and in any other era of Cuban history he would himself be just that: an illiterate black peasant.

The coach carries us back to the hotel via Revolution Square, a vast open space in which Fidel delivers his three-hour speeches to an audience of a quarter of a million. On one side of the square stands the Ministry of Defence, heavily guarded by soldiers in steel helmets, and on another side the headquarters of the Central Committee of the Communist Party. In the coach I ask Carlos whether he is a member of the Communist Party.

'Not yet,' he says. 'It is not easy, you know. But if I work well ...'

Let us consider, briefly, the political history of the Cuban Revolution since that first day of January 1959, when Batista took wing with his henchmen, and the Castroite forces entered Havana. Up to that moment Castro had never spoken as a Marxist. He was welcomed by the progressive middle class as the young leader of a revolution which would be democratic and 'social'—a vague notion which usually promises more than it yields. In 1953 Castro had called for the restoration of the democratic constitution framed in 1940, and this platform was reiterated in the Manifesto issued from the Sierra Maestra in July 1957, which contained a formal promise of free elections at the end of one year, an 'absolute guarantee' of a free Press, and the granting of all individual rights guaranteed by the 1940 Constitution. But on 1 May 1960, more than a year after he took power as Prime Minister, he described electoral democracy as a corrupt and fraudulent betrayal of the people. Naturally, many of his most sincere followers believed that he had betrayed *them*. He, in turn, castigated them for their petty-bourgeois prejudices. By 1961 all those who believed in electoral democracy had been ousted from power and many of them had gone into exile.

Castro's about-turn has been interpreted in three different ways. First, there are those who argue that he was a secret Marxist all along and simply disguised the fact in order to maximize his support. On at least one occasion Fidel himself has claimed that this is so; but, on balance, it is unlikely. Secondly, there are those who argue that he was corrupted by power in the classical pattern; once you hold all the reins in your hands, why put them at risk? There is surely some truth in this view. But Castro is not corrupted by power in the sense which applies to the majority of Latin American dictators. He does not use power to enrich himself, to open Swiss bank accounts, to buy real estate abroad, or to further the fortunes of his family. Right or wrong, he is a fanatical idealist; he believes implicitly in his own judgment; and he finds it almost impossible to believe that a politician who could oppose either him or his programme in an election could be honest, sincere, or truly dedicated to the wellbeing of the Cuban masses. And, it must be admitted, elections in a country like Cuba are deeply divisive; they institutionalize conflict and coalesce personal ambitions into factions. Finally, it would be naïve to assume that any election, let alone one in Cuba, merely reflects the will of the people, or the majority. Elections also have to do with money; and once the Castro régime had embarked on agrarian reform and the expropriation of foreign enterprises, there is no doubt where American money would have gone.

The September 1973 military coup and counter-revolution in Chile at first sight confirms this analysis. A Marxist President, constitutionally elected, attempted to implement a radical programme of economic reform and nationalization within the rule of law. As a consequence, American corporation money was thrown into the struggle against him while the entrepreneurial classes of Chile openly sabotaged economic life—of course, workers do the same when outraged—thus precipitating a state of inflation and chaos which compelled Salvador Allende to rely increasingly on emergency expedients. Quoting these as violations of the constitution, the armed forces snuffed out the light and smashed the candle. At the same time, Allende's refusal to employ revolutionary methods to achieve revolutionary results had provoked extreme leftists to embark on non-constitutional campaigns of their own—notably forcible land-seizures. Nevertheless, before one interprets these events as vindicating Castroism, one should note two factors. First, Allende never commanded the support of more than half the Chilean electorate, and sometimes less. Secondly, whereas Castro inherited a power vacuum, Allende took office with the armed forces in sound order. Had he attempted to transform Chile into a 'popular democracy' or to suppress the opposition, his bloody downfall might have come sooner.

The third school of interpretation regards Castro's turn-about as the child of circumstances. Once American enmity had become implacable and Soviet support indispensable, could the Cuban leaders do anything but copy the Soviet model of government? Yet the Cuban political system is by no means a carbon copy of the Soviet one. An attractive anecdote, which may or may not be apocryphal, runs like this: At the United Nations, Castro meets Gomulka of Poland and Novotny of Czechoslovakia. In the style of elder statesmen, they lead this brash young man aside. 'Look,' says Gomulka, 'the Americans want you to hold elections and you are only making trouble for yourself by not holding them.' Novotny agrees. 'You'll get 99.6 per cent of the vote. We always do.'

Fidel strokes his beard, ponders, then shakes his head. 'And you are really satisfied with 99.6 per cent?'

The fact is, at any stage Castro could have held rigged elections and emerged with a huge plurality. But he despises rigged elections even more than free ones! Did Jesus ever ask his followers to *elect* him Son of God?

But Castro does not turn the other cheek. Those who protested were treated as traitors; the more devoted their loyalty in the past, the more heinous their treason. Such was the case with Hubert Matos, an intellectual who had fought alongside Castro in the Sierra Maestra and subsequently been appointed Governor of Camagüey Province. Alarmed, like others, by the rapid growth of Communist influence within Cuba and by the pro-Communist leanings of Fidel's brother Raúl, in October 1959 he wrote to Castro expressing his desire to resign. 'Everyone who has spoken frankly to you about the Communist problem has had to leave or be dismissed ... It is wrong to treat those who want to discuss serious problems as reactionary conspirators.' Castro's prompt reaction was to do just that. Matos and thirty-four of his officers were brought before a court in which Castro himself virtually played the roles of prosecutor, witness, and judge. Matos was sentenced to twenty years in prison, five more than Castro himself had received after his abortive attack on the Moncada Barracks in 1953. But whereas Castro was released after twenty-two months, Matos remains in prison after fourteen years. Probably Matos was innocent of the main charges brought against him; true or not, he is the victim of an autocrat's implacable spirit of vengeance.

The political leadership which had emerged in Cuba by 1961 was essentially a coalition of disparate elements. Castro's own 26 July Movement, founded in 1954, began to fade into oblivion by 1960. In July 1961 it was merged with the Revolutionary Directorate, an urban student movement which had succeeded in seizing the Presidential Palace and Havana University as Batista's empire collapsed. (One of its leaders, Fauré Chomón, became Cuba's first Ambassador to the Soviet Union.) As for the old Communist Party, founded in 1925 and latterly known as the Popular Socialist Party, it had only belatedly supported Castro's guerrilla movement. Its veteran leaders, obedient for years to Moscow, had little in common with the bearded, ardent, impetuous young men who had committed their lives to an armed struggle against overwhelmingly superior forces. The Popular Socialist Party was strictly urban and quite small; in 1959 it had about seventeen thousand members. But its leaders possessed administrative experience and organizational cunning which Castro needed, particularly if he was to persuade the Russians that they were not pouring money and resources down the drain. In December 1961 he thanked the Communists for having rescued the Revolution from its amateurish confusion. By October 1965 he had emerged as the leader (general secretary) of a new, unitary Cuban Communist Party.

And yet it would be wrong to assume that Castro was really taken over by the old Communists. Admittedly some of them tried it, but they burned their fingers. The sheer speed of agrarian and urban reform, let alone the wholesale nationalization of foreign enterprises, was achieved by disregarding their pleas for caution, their grumbling opposition. When a leading Communist, Aníbal Escalante, tried to build up a power machine of his own, Castro gave him a public tongue-lashing and drove him out of Cuba. When Escalante, having returned, tried it yet again, he and eight other former PSP leaders were imprisoned in 1968 after a trial in which Castro once again played all the parts, and in which the defence was deprived of all customary rights, including the right to address the court. Escalante got fifteen years' hard labour for a crime which does not feature in the Criminal Code—forming a 'micro-faction'.

When one says 'customary rights' one must remember that the basic right of habeas corpus had disappeared in 1960, despite protests from the Lawyers' Association and the Havana University Law Faculty. In 1965 Castro himself put the number of political prisoners at twenty thousand (exiles claim forty thousand), and by 1970 there had been about five thousand politically motivated executions. Twenty thousand political prisoners in Cuba represents a percentage equivalent to half a million in the United States. The old Cuban legal profession has been completely smashed and nowadays minor offences are dealt with by Tribunales Populares (of which there were three hundred and sixty-six in 1968), whose judges must be good Communists with at least a Sixth Grade education.

The Communist Party which today rules Cuba remains essentially an instrument of Castro's personal prestige and power. Constantly he shifts the balance of power ... now the Party holds it, now the militia, now the Army. The Party itself is small and selective—in 1970 it had only seventy-eight thousand members. Carlos must wait. Despite promises, no National Congress of the Party has ever been held; in theory the Central Committee is elected by the National Congress, but in fact it is nominated by Fidel. Within the ruling politburo and secretariat the old Communists have never been allowed to gain decisive influence, and Castro has not spared their feelings in loudly castigating the Moscow-oriented CPs of Latin America for their cowardly compromises. (Indeed, certain Cuban Communists once held office under Batista, and Fidel doesn't let them forget it.)

Peering out of the bedroom window the following morning I

find the sky overcast and my skull being pierced by a band of steel needles. I swallow a couple of Paracetamol and go down to breakfast feeling slightly less of a hypochondriac.

'You don't look so well,' Carlos remarks.

'I haven't slept very well since we arrived.'

He nods. 'The adjustment is not easy.'

After breakfast Rafael prods his Soviet engine into life and we roar away through now-familiar streets to visit one of the houses of ex-President Batista outside Havana. Or so it transpires, since the main objective, a small bungalow converted into a museum of the fight against illiteracy, turns out to be locked and bolted. We sit in the shade while Carlos goes in search of the caretaker, and we are still sitting in the shade when, half an hour later, Carlos comes back without the caretaker. Apparently his energies have been commandeered by a volunteer labour battalion.

Batista's villa is nothing to write home about, but across the courtyard is a gymnasium once patronized by the dictator's officers and now used by the local militia. Wall-bars, volley balls, boxers' bags, wooden vaulting-horses, fencing foils, ropes, pulleys, mats—quite honestly, *compañero*, I've seen all this at school and when I, too, was a soldier, and if you ever visit England, *compañero*, I do promise not to take you on a ten-mile journey to visit a tennis court. Meanwhile, I will use my imagination to fill the void, to sniff the lingering evil, as once I did as a boy in Edinburgh, when Hitler's yacht came to the harbour of Leith and we filed through the Führer's cabin where the upholstery still retained the aroma of Göring's cigars. But the gymnasium smells only of antiseptic and sweat—presumably the militia's.

Batista, of course, was not Hitler, and he was probably no worse than many other Latin American dictators. But he did symbolize perfectly that familiar degeneration from reforming rebel to greedy potentate which has so often made mock of Latin American idealism and which the United States, it must be admitted, observes with a foxy smile. The two ambassadors who represented the United States in Havana from 1953 to 1959, Arthur Gardner and Earl Smith, were devoted supporters of Batista; Smith, a confidant of Kennedy, was sounding the alarm bells about Castro even before Castro (or Kennedy) came to power. Until March 1958 Batista's officers were trained by an American military mission, and all necessary military equipment was furnished by the US. In 1957 a high-ranking US General went to Cuba to decorate with the Legion of Merit General Francisco Tabernilla, Cuban Chief of Staff, Commander of the Air Force, and a strong exponent of bombing civilian populations into a proper state of discipline. As for the American Press, it had little to say about the brutality of the régime. Batista was a reliable anti-Communist and a reliable protector of American economic investments; Wall Street and Washington asked no more than that.

But when Batista's principal henchmen, the *Batistianos*, were put on trial and executed, there was suddenly a great outcry in the United States. The trials were held in front of three judges and without a jury, although the defendants were allowed counsel. With one exception (after which a re-trial was held), they were conducted with gravity and decorum, and were very far from the frenzied, lynch-law, kangaroo courts the American public believed them to be. On the other hand, Castro showed himself capable of intervening to reverse a verdict which acquitted some of Batista's pilots for lack of evidence. Sympathetic foreign observers like C. Wright Mills echoed the official Cuban view that the timely execution of five or six hundred *Batistianos* saved Cuba from a bloodbath. Whether true or not, foreign critics must remember that revolution and civil war are not a general election; that Cuba has never been a country which can accommodate Her Majesty's Loyal Opposition; that in

1945 the victorious Allies made up their own *post hoc* crimes and punishments in response to what their peoples had suffered; and, finally, that the American politicians most piously horrified by the trials of the *Batistianos* had been very far from horrified by General Franco's reprisals against Spanish Republicans.

I am glowering at a vaulting-horse in Hamlet-like mood. What is more painful, comic, and humiliating than to rush at a vaulting-horse, leap—and land on top of it with a crucified groin? I back away, climb a rope. Carlos laughs and does the same. The sky outside is black with thunder, fork lightning swoops from the sky, the trees bend under the wind, and torrential rain descends. Inches deep within seconds, it floods under the glass doors of the gymnasium. The staff calmly sweep it back through storm holes into the basement. We are served coffee in a small room lined with photos of the Soviet Grand Master and former World Champion, Tigran Petrosian, playing a simultaneous chess tournament in Havana. Che Guevara is one of his humble opponents. Gazing thoughtfully at his board, playing black, and wearing his trademark beret, Che has moved his pawn to K4. Any of us might do the same! It is a pleasure to have shared at least one thought, one simple gambit, with this remarkable man.

The storm blows away as abruptly as it arrived and we drive back to the hotel through flooded streets. The rains have washed the persistent aroma of seaweed out of the air. Along the Malecon boys are flying kites or fishing from the rocks which line the shore between the breakers and the sea wall. The daily Soviet oil-tanker is cautiously edging its passage out of the harbour towards the open sea and the American frigates lurking beyond the horizon. Not for the first time we pass a new hospital which has risen ten floors then comes to a ragged halt; cranes, scaffolding, and pulleys hang from it, its base is surrounded by piles of sand, cement-mixers and pre-cast concrete blocks, but not a construction worker is in sight: perhaps they have gone away to plant coffee.

After lunch there was to be a special visit to a special film at a special cinema, a treat which gained in anticipation from the faint aura of mystery surrounding it. But Carlos wearily announces that the special cinema is closed 'temporarily' and that the afternoon is therefore 'free'. The groans are loud, particularly from the older folk whose feet are already blistered enough. Martha and I are on our indignant way upstairs when Carlos beckons to us discreetly, almost furtively. As we follow him out of the hotel and round a corner, he hurries ahead of us, offering not a word in explanation. A small Maserati is parked, its engine idling and two young men seated in front. The one in the passenger seat jumps out, tilts his seat forward, and indicates with a gesture that we should climb in the back. Too late to send a telegram, too late to phone the British Consulate, in such cases it's always too late, they make sure of that. Poor Martha: she at least is innocent, but how can I persuade them?

Obviously my face mirrors my thoughts for Carlos is suddenly convulsed with laughter and his arm is squeezing my shoulder reassuringly. As the Maserati slithers nimbly through side-streets the three Cubans never stop laughing until they abruptly do, suddenly sad and reproachful that I should have entertained so distorted a picture of their country and its natural hospitality. At some stage during our unfathomable journey Carlos introduces us: our four hands move in a multiple embrace rather like the end of a doubles match in tennis, except that my partner and I forget to shake hands.

We disembark at the Havana Libre and descend smartly into a dark, windowless bar. It being mid-afternoon we are spared the deafening services of musicians. A waiter comes to our table and it's drinks all round and welcome to Cuba:

our glasses go up to that. Carlos explains that these bright-
eyed young men, Juan and Francisco, not only work for the
news agency Prensa Latina, but are also old friends of his
from schooldays. Juan has worked as a journalist in Paris
and Moscow; having heard from Carlos that I am a writer,
he had suggested a meeting at the first opportunity. We all
nod enthusiastically and light cigarettes; Martha coaxes
them into accepting her Virginians, and I slowly adjust
myself to the honour of meeting Cubans with access to a
car. But why did they bring us here to the Havana Libre?
Obviously, Martha will later reason, because if we had
remained in the Deauville other members of our party might
have concluded that we were being granted favours. Or to
evade Nicole, perhaps? Is the French girl, with her too-
ready responses, her ultra-orthodoxy, perhaps a pain in the
neck to the Cubans?

'What brought you to Cuba?' Juan asks. Carlos translates.
Juan has some French but it's a few years since he was in
Paris and he doesn't trust it.

'That's a big question! Curiosity? Admiration? You
know ...'

'But what are your impressions, please? I realize you have
not been here long ... are things as you expected?'

Francisco and Carlos hang on my reply not, I suspect,
because they are so concerned with my impressions, but because my expectations, if accurately revealed, will give
them a window on the current West European image of
Cuba.

And so, for a while, we chat amiably. They tell me a
number of things I do not know and these I shamelessly jot
down on a scrap of old paper for later transcription into
my notebook. But nothing Martha or I say seems likely to
budge the journalistic hands of Juan and Francisco from
their cigarettes and Havana Club Drys.

The question of wages crops up. Workers' wages and

peasants' wages, you understand. But what of Juan's wage, and Francisco's, and Carlos's, too, since we are about it? Well—Francisco beckons to the waiter and it's more drinks all round—there seems to be some reluctance here to reveal personal wages. It is not quite clear to me whether in Cuba one loses face among friends because one's remuneration is too low or too high.

'And this car you drive, is it yours personally?'

'No, no, naturally not. It belongs to Prensa Latina.'

I ask them about their work; do they consider themselves to be working at this moment, for example? They glance at each other warily; what is this fellow getting at? Juan explains that he is currently employed providing foreign correspondents in Havana with information and news about events in Cuba; Francisco expects to depart for Santiago de Chile within a few weeks to report back on the Chilean road to socialism. Now what can I have meant by asking whether they are working *now*? Embarrassed, I explain unconvincingly that a free-lance writer is forever taking mental notes —even when he is drinking a Havana Club Dry, he is trying to find the right words for the drift of the lemon peel across the sinking surface of the liquid.

They nod politely.

Yes, Juan is married, but not Francisco.

We are all lacquered, now, in a peculiarly Cuban torpor. It hardly seems worth a kidnapping. I notice my legs straightening out, which is always a sign.

'Of course you have no constitution here in Cuba, written or unwritten?'

They sit up a bit. A bleep on the morse code of international tension.

'We have the Fundamental Law,' Juan says.

'Do you think that Cuban socialism will become more democratic—I mean, in formal, institutional ways?'

Carlos translates from French into Spanish. There is then

some debate among themselves in Spanish, perhaps about the meaning of my question, perhaps about the meaning of their reply.

'Yes, but what exactly do you mean?' Juan says. (He seems to enjoy some seniority or merely personal preponderance over Francisco.)

'Like an elected legislative assembly,' I suggest. 'Or like an elected National Congress of the Party.'

'I think that each country must tread its own road to socialism,' Juan says. Both Carlos and Francisco endorse that.

'Why answer in formulas? Do all journalists in Cuba speak like politicians or like manuals for Young Pioneers? Can one really talk of socialism where there is no collective decision-making?'

Juan sits up very straight now and lights another cigarette. 'Listen,' he says in a voice suddenly doubled in force, 'every major decision in Cuba has been made after a thorough discussion at all levels. Immediate tasks and priorities are explained to our people in far greater detail than in your country, for example.'

'Explained, certainly. But are the people consulted? Do the peasants really administer their own co-operatives, or the workers their own factories?'

'Such things take time,' Juan says. 'But our people are very rapidly gaining in maturity.'

'If you had lived here,' says Carlos, 'you would have found the change that has taken place within a few years quite astonishing.'

The three Cubans flick ash off their cigarettes in salute to that thought.

I mention a report that since August 1968 the working population has carried labour cards, on which blemishes of absenteeism or indiscipline are recorded. Had not the Russians in their time done the same?

Cordiality is now on the wane. A contemporary Cuban is never sure whether he should proudly accept Cuba's debt to the 'first socialist state' or indignantly repudiate the suggestion that Cuba's chosen path is anything but indigenous.

'We encounter the same problem with so many Western visitors,' Juan says.

'What problem?'

'On the one hand they desire Cuba to be quite different from their own countries. On the other hand they get upset if it isn't exactly the same.'

Martha and I laugh in agreement. We all smile our way into a milder zone. Jokes are exchanged about those crazy enough to write for a living. I explain that like any good Cuban socialist I send my wife out to work, and Martha is then called upon to explain the nature of her work as an editor for a London publisher. Up to this point the Cubans have addressed all their remarks to me alone in a closed circle of masculine mental virtuosity, but heavyweight conclusions should not be drawn from this; Cuba is spilling over with professional women who have plenty to say for themselves and who insist on being heard. Reconstructed Cuban men do listen respectfully, but with a hint of that bemused resignation found among American college professors who for the first time in their lives must pay attention to student opinions on matters about which students were traditionally expected to have none.

Juan peels off and Francisco drops us at the Deauville. But we have bitten into only two hours of the afternoon and our 'freedom' still confronts us by the time-acre. We take a bus and head for a movie. On this occasion Martha is wearing a long skirt down to her ankles, thus provoking fascinated attention; these ex-Spaniards are not sure whether they're witnessing the reincarnation of Carmen or Lohengrin. As good revolutionaries, they're perturbed by any semblance of the unusual.

Though it is mid-week there is a queue outside the cinema and the auditorium is packed. We get in at one peso per head. The film, *No tenemos derecho a esperar* ('We Don't Have the Right to Wait'), has been much recommended in the Press and the première was attended by Castro himself. Directed by Rogelio Paris in splendid colour, it is essentially an agitational documentary dealing with Cuba's recent construction achievements. The audience around us watches in intent and appreciative silence as the widescreen unfolds a rich panorama of new housing projects, dams, roads, schools, technical institutes, power plants, milking stations, fertilizer plants, and hospitals.

Doctors, dentists, clinics, and hospitals in Cuba are now free. This may not appeal to the American Medical Association, but it appeals to the Cubans. In Cuba one moves among an abundantly healthy population, and this is a tremendous tribute to the régime. In 1958, the budget of the Ministry of Public Health was twenty-two million pesos; in 1968, it was two hundred and sixty-three million. In 1958, there were forty-four hospitals in Cuba; in 1968, there were two hundred and twenty-one. Polyclinics increased from zero in 1958 to two hundred and sixty in 1968. The number of available hospital beds doubled to forty-two thousand. But, because so many doctors emigrated, and because a qualified doctor cannot be produced overnight, the number of practising physicians has increased only very marginally to seven thousand. Poliomyelitis, which used to claim on average three hundred victims a year, is now virtually eliminated. The same is true of malaria, which used to run to several thousand cases a year. Deaths from diphtheria and gastroenteritis have been halved, and typhoid has also been held down. But for some reason infant mortality, at forty per thousand, remains not only static, but above the Caribbean average.

Industrial construction is not a favourite subject for

British or American film directors, nor for their audiences. We know all about it; it's a bore. In any case we have so much of it that we feel threatened, we are worried about pollution and ecological balance, and we will fight to keep a green field green. Not so in Cuba. Here the creation of a sound industrial infrastructure is greeted with rapturous enthusiasm. I like this film. The music is good and the commentary is sparse, allowing the camera (often airborne) to speak for itself. It is also a film full of typical Cuban faces, and what comes out of those faces (to me) is a calm and determined pride. But I suppose it is deceptive in one sense: Soviet aid to Cuba is worth a million dollars a day, but the film seems to be telling the Cubans that they have achieved all this by their own efforts.

No tenemos derecho a esperar ends on a triumphant note and the lights come up in the large, air-conditioned auditorium to reveal rows of black and white faces, serene and satisfied.

'I think I've caught the Cuban bug: a rapid oscillation between enthusiasm and apathy.'

'But you're always like that,' Martha says.

Next comes a newsreel, a genre which has almost died out in the West under the impact of television. The main subject —the sole subject—is Vietnam. First, a loaded prelude: Nazi war criminals writhing in guilt (poker-faced actually) at Nuremberg. Then hand-held shots of North Vietnamese peasants wading knee-deep in mud in an attempt to repair the damaged dikes; glimpses of American bombers; cut to devastated hospitals and schools. Now the good Americans: Jane Fonda, Ramsey Clark, flashbulbs, microphones. Cut to frontal confrontation with Nixon himself, all jowl and grisly sincerity, unnervingly speaking in a Spanish voice several quavers higher than his own. The audience does not hiss. Voice over: *Venceremos!* Blackout.

Delighted, I rehearse a small sermon castigating the cheap,

trivial, escapist rubbish served up to Western movie audiences ... But wait; the programme, evidently, is by no means concluded. The lights dim and prancing credits cavort across the screen in the coy idiom of musical notation. The audience stirs, straightens its back, bubbles with pleasurable anticipation. What can it be? Alas, a glossy Spanish movie portraying the glamorous existence of a star Madrid footballer who has invested in a pop group and false eyelashes. Zooming around fabulous Madrid/fabulous Costa Brava/ fabulous cardboard sets in an open Mercedes, sleek and suntanned in his fabulous all-white gear, he and his swinging companions burst into the latest hit tunes to the unending joy of casual passers-by who are left stunned on the sidewalk, humming with happiness. Kiss kiss. As we pick our way through the legs and out of the darkened auditorium, we leave behind us a Cuban audience lost in wonder.

'Don't look so glum,' Martha says. 'We can't all be highbrows.'

'Highbrows!'

It would be nice, right now, to sit down at a pavement café, order a coffee or a Daiquiri, light a cigarette, and debate this whole issue. But where? There are benches in the squares, under the trees, but Daiquiris don't gush out of fountains. In the hotel lobby we stare moodily for a moment at the night-and-day television set (the programme is makeshift and the reception poor), take a free copy of the Government newspaper *Granma* from the rack, enter the elevator, gulp iced water in our room. I twiddle with the knob of the radio.

'How about a swim?' Martha suggests.

'You go.'

She pads out to get brown and wet. I open *Granma* (it is translated into English and French in its weekly editions) and I groan. An official Communist newspaper is just one long Government Press-conference, a casserole of slogans and ex-

72

hortations. Work harder ... now is the time ... women! ...
solidarity in the face of imperialist aggression/barbarism/
crimes ... joint-communiqué ... the friendship of the two
peoples ... Fidel says ...

Granma is not the only paper to appear in Cuba. There is
also *Juventud Rebelde*, the organ of the Young Communists'
League; its cultural supplement, *El Caíman Barbudo*; the
magazine *Unión*; the satirical weekly *Palante*; and there
also exist magazines of special interest to women like *Mujeres*
and *Romances*. The theoretical organ, *Cuba socialista*, has
been in a state of suppressed limbo since February 1967,
apparently waiting for the Central Committee of the Party
to decide what socialist theory should be.

When we in the West speak or boast of a free Press we
often do so carelessly and without justification. At many
breakfast tables in the United States a family which does not
like the single local paper has to read the stories on the corn-
flakes packet. Even if the media in the United States are not
intimidated by the Government, most of them are certainly
intimidated by their advertisers or sponsors. At all levels,
money speaks too loudly. Nevertheless, I do feel convinced
that an imperfect plurality is better than none. Apparently
Fidel, too, once believed this (in the days when he was
assuring American newspaper editors that capitalism falls
short on justice, and Communism on freedom). On 29 April
1959 he said on television: 'If one begins to close down *one*
newspaper no other newspaper will feel safe—and if one
begins to persecute *one* person because of his political views
nobody else can feel safe.' But the pressures on recalcitrant
editors mounted. The union of journalists and the union of
graphic workers, militants of the Revolution, began to insert
comments criticizing reactionary articles. These were
known as *coletillas*, or little tails.

During 1960 the 'free Press' died in Cuba. (An extraordinarily large number of newspapers had been published

73

under Batista, most of them surviving by accepting subsidies from the Government.) In January 1960 *Avance* was taken over by its staff and later closed down. The Government took over *Prensa libre*. The conservative *Diario de la Marina* was seized by an armed gang after the majority of the staff had supported the publisher's right to criticize the Government. The liberal daily *El Mundo* was confiscated. In August, the celebrated weekly journal *Bohemia*, with a circulation of over six hundred thousand, was expropriated. The publication of the daily *Informacíon* ceased in December. All Cuban Governments had manipulated the Press by means of bribery, and the monthly budget for this operation under Batista was a quarter of a million dollars, but the control achieved was relative, not absolute. Henceforward it was to be absolute.

What is *Granma* like? It is short—short of hard news, short of paper. The concept of news without a framework of propaganda is unacceptable to it. Only one side of an argument is allowed. The paper exudes a constant spirit of exhortation. Here is a not untypical headline dated 19 May 1968: 'We have accepted the challenge of nature and victory will depend on our organizational capacity in this struggle.' Accompanying photographs depict officials and their audience at a provincial meeting of the Party to plan a local economic offensive. On another page a headline urges: 'Let us reinforce work discipline during the revolutionary offensive.' Bulldozers are seen advancing in the desert regions of Pinar del Río.

At the same time, the paper exudes a particular kind of piety. 'May Day guests visit Che Guevara Brigade in Camagüey.' Or: 'We are constantly becoming more alert, more conscientious.' Or: 'Workers from the Ministry of the Food Industry—working voluntarily—built a school in ten days.' Or: 'More than three thousand students from the University of Oriente and a large number of faculty members and other

University personnel left for the northern part of the province, where they will remain until the end of the month
doing agricultural work.' Or: 'Nicaro workers set new
monthly production record: two thousand tons of nickel-
cobalt processed in April.' (Plus an exciting photo of a crane
hoisting minerals.)

Events become standardized after being processed through
ritual phrases and formulas. 'During his stay in our country,
the Minister of Foreign Relations of Sierra Leone placed a
wreath at the foot of the José Martí monument.' After
which, 'the two parties were in complete accord ... Both
sides expressed their support ... verified their essential
identity of opinion ...' And why? Because of, apparently,
'the people of Cuba's absolute confidence in the increasing
development of the important political, economic, social and
cultural transformations that are taking place in Sierra
Leone.'

In London the editors of the tabloids, the *Sun* and the
Daily Mirror, compete for readers by showing more and
more pretty girls, by filling whole pages with horoscopes,
by predicting royal weddings and by relegating serious news
to a few, stifled centre pages. And yet, in a sense, these
editors display more respect for their readers than do their
Cuban colleagues who churn out balderdash of the sort
quoted above. I do not for a moment deny that the Press
has, or should have, a serious mission to educate its readers,
to raise the level of their interests, to awaken their social
consciousness, and to bring them exemplary news of heroes
and martyrs. In a sense *Granma* undertakes such worthy
tasks, but in so transparently a manipulative manner that
even those Cubans who have never heard of Sierra Leone
must ultimately demand to be addressed like adults.

After dinner we drift down to the bar—Carlos, the two
coach drivers, Nicole, the Young Swiss, Martha and I. A
group of elderly black musicians does its best to make con-

versation impossible, but we shout doggedly through a caco-
phony which can have changed very little since the days
when the bar was propped up by Americans. Martha asks
Carlos whether he is married. Yes, and he lives with his wife
and small son in the Varadero district of Havana. Thereupon
Rafael and Pedro proudly produce snapshots of their own
families, tuck them back in their wallets, and settle down to
an evening's drinking in the Deauville.

'You men should be with your families,' Nicole says. To
Martha she adds: 'Cubans are still male chauvinists at heart.'
Carlos seems rather abashed but is forced to translate by
Rafael, who, getting the message, looks delighted. He winks
broadly at me as if to say: 'I can see *you* understand the
ways of the world.' He then asks Carlos what I do for a
living. On hearing that I am a writer, he guffaws, slaps me on
the back, calls me 'Eming-way' and 'good fellow' and orders
drinks all round. (An act of which the Young Swiss alone is
incapable—when my second turn comes, I cut him out; he
blinks owlishly and orders himself a beer in a fog of blighted
egoism.)

'Eming-way good, eh?' says Rafael.

'Very good.'

'Very rich, Eming-way. You rich, eh?'

'No.'

'No?' Rafael winks roguishly at the others. 'You not
good writer, eh?'

'I'm afraid not.'

Rafael puts an arm protectively round Martha's shoulder,
but then his English fails him and he lapses into silence at
the prospect of the palaver of translation. Carlos remarks
that Hemingway had lived in Cuba, that his house is now a
museum, and that with luck we may be able to visit it. (No
such luck; museum closed, caretaker gone to cut sugar, etc.)
The conversation, inevitably, drifts round to the subject of
America. Learning that Martha was born there and that I

have spent a couple of years in the States, Carlos grimaces good-humouredly and remarks: 'I suppose many good things happen there, and many bad things.'

Rafael and Pedro nod soberly. Many good things, many bad.

But this jogging limbo of rum and nostalgia is not to Nicole's taste. She likes a fight.

'What are your politics really?' she asks me, stressing that 'really' as if I had been engaged in an elaborate subterfuge. Carlos considers the question so important (he has not mentioned our afternoon interview with the two journalists) that he translates for the benefit of Rafael and Pedro (ever the Silent One). Even the musicians break off their lung-stretching labours to hear the answer.

'I'm a Scandinavian social democrat.'

'You mean your family comes from Sweden?' Carlos asks.

'No more than yours comes from Russia.'

Nicole finds this remark irritating. A provocation, no less. She helps out the confused Cubans by explaining that I am confessing my adherence to 'petty-bourgeois reformism and vacillation'.

Rafael pretends to look shocked, but there is a twinkle in his eye. I assure him that Eming-way, too, was really a Scandinavian social democrat. Rafael thumps my back, man-to-man; these women...

'In Cuba,' explains Carlos, 'we have to fight against all forms of revisionism and opportunism.'

'That's always a formula for giving anyone hell at a moment's notice; for suddenly setting desk clerks to work making *papier mâché* anatomies for schools; or for scalping homosexuals.'

'Capitalist ideology,' says Nicole, 'is selectively sentimental.'

Martha looks unhappy. Carlos groans at the developing friction, but also because understanding is the hardest of all

77

crops to harvest. 'You must understand ...' he says ...

You must understand our past. You must understand that by 1959 United States investments in Cuba were worth one thousand million dollars; that Americans owned at least six hundred companies; that seven per cent of the national product was accounted for by salaries and wages paid by these firms; that twenty per cent of the national budget derived from the taxes they paid; that 69·8 per cent of Cuban imports came from the US and 66·8 per cent of exports went to the US. These were the days when Earl Smith told the Senate that normally the American Ambassador was the second most important person in Cuba, and sometimes more important than the Cuban President himself. It was an American journalist, Tad Szulc of the *New York Times*, who wrote in April 1960: 'For the fifty-seven years of its independence, Cuba has lived more as an appendage of the United States than as a sovereign nation.' Of course, American investment is also high in Canada. But Canada does not suffer from a single-crop economy; the Canadian Government, which has no need to grant ruinous concessions, is willing and able to tax foreign corporations at a realistic level in order to engender capital investment across the economy. But in Cuba, the US-owned Electric Company, while enjoying a monopoly position, declined to take the investment risk of extending electricity supplies to the countryside. Agrarian reform of any sort was out of the question without a thumbs-up from the American sugar-plantation companies, and their thumbs remained down. Castro put it this way: 'Our nation was subjected to sixty years of political, economic, and cultural asphyxia ... What is Cuba's history but that of Latin America? What is the history of Latin America but the history of Asia, Africa, and Oceania? And what is the history of all these peoples but the history of cruellest exploitation of the world by imperialism?'

78

And what does a 'Scandinavian social democrat' say to that?

He might add that economic penetration of the sort described certainly deforms development, but it also generates the development it deforms. It distributes wealth unjustly, but it also creates the wealth which the Revolution can redistribute. For better or for worse, Western society has transcended the agrarian economy by the road of commercial and industrial capitalism.

What do ordinary Cubans really feel about America and the Americans? So monolithically hostile towards the United States is official Cuban propaganda that it is difficult to separate rhetoric from feeling, the posture from the true sentiment. To those Cubans who support the Socialist Revolution, the US is first and foremost an incomparably rich and powerful neighbour, whose implacable hostility signifies the perpetual imminence of an armed attack. At the same time, the 'new Cuban' has to come to terms not only with the White House, the State Department and the Pentagon, but also with a force which is more pervasive, more amorphous, more insidious, and more personally felt— the American way of life. By that I mean a high standard of living; the free-enterprise style of grab and gain; the dollar, the movie star, Coca-Cola, the camera, and the baseball World Series; the inherent disdain felt by many Americans of north European origin for the Latins; racism; the bewildering blend of genuine freedom and corruption which characterizes North American political life. In a sense all Cubans, except the youngest generation, are familiar with the American way of life. Before 1959 it moulded and scarred the native Cuban landscape; it pulled young Cubans eager for advancement to American universities and business enterprises; and, finally, after the Revolution, it tugged more than half a million Cubans back into exile. Most town-based Cubans have a relative or a friend who opted for America rather than for Castro, and so the great enemy remains also a great magnet—lynching allegiance, confronting conflicting values, juxtaposing private ambition with national loyalty, splitting families. For these reasons one must ultimately conclude that a *rapprochement* between the two countries would release within Cuba a dam of pent-up goodwill, of curiosity, and of proud hospitality.

It must be a healthy sign that the Cubans are no longer prepared to offer hospitality to the psychopaths, bank robbers, and unhappy lovers who pluck aeroplanes out of the sky at gunpoint.

The next day Carlos confirms that this is to be our last in Havana before beginning our tour of the island. At the end of our trip we will spend a few more days in the capital and Carlos very much hopes that by that time special cinemas, illiteracy museums, the Hemingway Museum, etc., will all be open. A general murmur from the four tables endorses this hope.

We are eating well, if a little monotonously. Rice crops up regularly for lunch and dinner and beer is always available. A very good meal might consist of jerked pork, rice, peas, wild salad, *chocho*, cheese, and stewed guava. Eating always in the same dining-room in the same company imposes a mild feeling of claustrophobia, that weary sense of *déjà vu* which most families experience over the years. But, even if we had not paid for our meals in advance, the business of booking a table in one of the few available restaurants would consume all our time and energy, probably fruitlessly. Goaded by unmentionable appetites, the Young Swiss has spent a hot hour queueing outside the Coppelia ice-cream parlour (a graceful, pavilion-style building) in central Havana. At the Coppelia patience is eventually rewarded by a spectacular range of flavours: almond, vanilla, banana, coconut, guava, orange, mango, melon, pawpaw, pineapple, plantain, and even tomato. Enough to make your mouth water. The Young Swiss's mouth certainly watered, for he seems to have sampled them all, the sad consequences being that his stomach is in turmoil and his pale skin has turned the colour of an unripe tomato. American Express remedies having failed, the prospect of a long coach-journey on erratic socialist roads fills him with foreboding, and only desperation overcomes scepticism when Nicole offers him a string of large white tablets, home-grown. But socialist medicine works a miracle. By next morning the Young Swiss will be, as he puts it to me while borrowing a cigarette, 'all go-go'. To mark the occasion he purchases in the boutique a straw hat from which hence-forward he will be inseparable, despite Rafael's inexhaustible joy in slipping it from beneath the Young Swiss's chair during meals and placing it on the bald and oblivious head of the Old Swiss. We cross national frontiers, it seems, by the simplest routes.

Today the streets of Havana are charged with stress, with indignation, with lazy smiles, with banners and music and roaring lorries loaded with workers, with children running towards the carnival in ragged knots of interrupted motion, with girls in green uniforms whistling traffic into submission, with blaring loudspeakers and television screens bombarded by electronic exhortations. Cuba is about to demonstrate. It is five in the evening and half a million citizens of Havana surge towards the Havana Libre by foot, bus, and lorry, each segment of humanity neatly carved (only in the last moments does the neatness reveal itself) into the categories of Marxian lore: workers, peasants, shock brigades, volunteer brigades, Young Communists, women, Young Pioneers, the intelligentsia. It is 28 August 1972. At this moment (probably) bombs are falling in clusters of fire, high explosives, and fragmentation pellets on North Vietnam. We have gathered to protest.

The Cubans feel deeply for Vietnam. Two small peoples,

a common enemy, a Goliath. 1967 was officially named the Year of Heroic Vietnam (*año del Vietnam heroico*). The Castro Government has been critical of the Soviet Union for providing the Vietnamese with only limited assistance; since the Missile Crisis of 1962 the Cubans have not trusted the Russians' willingness to go to the limit. And Cuba, herself, of course, can do little to help so distant a friend; even when American troops landed in the Dominican Republic in April 1965, Cuba bellowed in helpless fury. Nevertheless, the sense of solidarity runs deep. Young Vietnamese Pioneers visit their Cuban counterparts, make pilgrimages to the guard-posts on the Guantánamo frontier, and exchange scarves. There are more than five hundred Vietnamese students attending Havana University, many of them studying electrical engineering and all of them working like beavers, particularly the girls, who achieve prodigious feats in the Spanish language in rapid time. Their Cuban professors unanimously praise their self-discipline, dedication, comradely approachability, and their 'excellent notes'.

The Cubans, meanwhile, have kept a hopeful eye on the Anti-War movement within the United States. Photographs of police beating up demonstrators in Miami are blown up, placarded, and pinned to lamp posts, fences, and buildings. The Cuban poet David Fernández (born 1940) has with obvious irony dedicated his 'A Song of Peace' to a Californian soldier killed in Vietnam:

> Perhaps you never thought
> It could happen.
> . . .
> Yet here you are, following after
> Others like yourself, who came
> To destroy the homes, the families,
> The budding hopes of this people,
> This people named Vietnam.

You probably never heard of it
Until that black day when they sent you,
Together with your buddies,
Without a word to tell you why,
Over to this land where now,
Undone by the very arms you brought along,
You are dying, dying, daily
Hopelessly and endlessly dying.*

An official rostrum has been erected on La Rampa, outside the high, grim façade of the Havana Libre. While the mass delegations move in a fairly orderly procession up the rectangular grid of roads leading to the flashpoint, the crowds on the sidewalks push and jostle in good-humoured anarchy, sporting home-made banners depicting Uncle Sam in every conceivable posture of physical discomfort and portraying Nixon (whose name even in the Cuban Press is spelt with a swastika replacing the 'x') as the Beast. The loudspeakers blare continuously, distant speeches are interspersed with choruses of patriotic songs, and heroic chants arise time and again from the multitude: *Cuba, si, Yanquis, no!* Inch by inch we manoeuvre our way towards the rostrum, halted by a solid wedge of people here, forcing a passage through a yielding corridor there, everyone going somewhere or standing still to watch everyone else. Finally, we catch a glimpse of the rostrum where Cuban leaders in green fatigues and Vietnamese officials in pyjama suits are seated side by side, their faces solemn and impassive, in one of those freakish alliances hewn out of the rock of international tension:

Cuba, si, Vietnam, si, Yanquis...
Venceremos! Venceremos!...
Patria o muerte! Patria o muerte!

*Translated by Claudia Beck. Literature printed in Cuba is no longer under copyright. Cuba has withdrawn from the international copyright convention, the better to pirate foreign literature.

Thunderous clapping. The great banners are raised again, reaching up towards the immense slogans draped from buildings.

Cuba, si...

But what, for me, is so odd, so dreamlike, so elusive about this gigantic demonstration of solidarity? Why do I, who am no stranger to political demonstrations, fail to connect? Then it strikes me: this is the first demo I have attended where the *Government* (damn it) is the sponsor! How unnatural! If Lewis Carroll were alive and well today, surely he would drop Alice down a hole into a world where, topsy-turvy, in defiance of all logic, the Government organized demos against itself! But wait a minute. The Cuban Government, by no stretch of the imagination Lewis Carroll, is merely an accomplished practitioner of the mass rally where the Government and the People are one in their struggle against a common enemy, and—equally unfamiliar to me—where those few policemen in evidence are regarded as friendly *compañeros* by the crowd. Demos are normally a forceful and dramatic way of saying 'No!' Certainly we are here to say 'No' to Nixon, 'No' to the Pentagon, but have we not really been brought together—the thought flickers—to say 'Yes' to Our Policy, 'Yes' to Our Leaders, 'Yes' to Our Revolution, 'Yes' to Us?

Yes, we have.

In my country, Carlos, one never says 'Yes'. Not unless one belongs to 'the silent majority', to the flaccid abdomen of the Gallup Poll.

But in my country, David, the majority is not silent.

Ah, yes.

The speeches continue. In Cuba how they continue. Trapped against the wall of a building under a cruel sun, deafened by the loudspeakers, by the incessant, irate outpouring of rhetoric, exhortation, and promises of victory, we fend off suffocation with elbows and knees, slowly fighting our way towards the fringes of the crowd where there is space to breathe, space to sit down. Here one encounters a gentle, patient apathy; a mosaic of private lives; a welded mass disintegrating into its atomic units, flirting, holding hands, taking pictures, staring at foreigners, waving to friends. Just living out the evening in the familiar aroma of political showbiz, being mildly entertained, leaning on the spectacular, star-gazing. Being together. In Cuba, it is not High Mass, not the Beatles, not the Pittsburgh Pirates, but this.

As we walk home along the Malecon the demonstrators are climbing into their trucks and buses, euphorically happy and proud as any festival's children could be. For us, Cuba has suddenly fulfilled her promise and we too are happy.

CHAPTER

3

Matanzas, Las Villas, Camagüey

We leave Havana on a broad, modern highway and head for Matanzas, some fifty miles to the east, along the north coast. Soon comes our first glimpse of sugar cane, green and upright, still well short of harvest time. We pass trucks loaded with farm workers, some in straw cowboy hats and others wearing the cotton peaked cap of the Revolution. They wave to us. We wave. Beside the road, horses and mules are tied to fences, gates, telegraph-poles. Cowboys are jogging easily in the saddle. In the province of Matanzas the rural population seems entirely white, entirely creole; only in the town will the blacks be seen again.

Modern geographers regard Cuba as an archipelago rather than as an island. Stretching some 745 miles west to east, with an average width of about 60 miles, Cuba is fringed by 1,600 keys, islands, and islets. The total area of 44,218 square miles is comparable to that of Pennsylvania. Located 98 miles from the Florida Keys, sitting astride the Gulf of Mexico, and the largest and most westerly of the Caribbean islands, it commands the sea approaches to Mexico, the Mississippi Valley and western Florida. (However, its own approaches are in turn commanded by the US Navy.) Some of the surrounding islands are uninhabited, while others support a few charcoal-burners and fishermen who catch fish, sponges, and crustaceans.

Cuba is a botanical garden. About eight thousand different species of trees and plants grow there. The climate is moderate and stable. The mean temperature is seventy-seven degrees Farenheit in winter, eighty degrees Farenheit in summer. July and August are the hottest months, but even then the temperature does not rise much above eighty degrees. Lying in the trade-wind belt, Cuba is ventilated by breezes from the northeast in summer and from the southeast in winter.

The dry season extends from November to April. The average rainfall in February is 1·48 inches, but in June it rises to 8·16 inches. From May until October, with some abatement in August, there are almost daily afternoon storms, many of considerable violence. In September and October tropical hurricanes are common. The provinces of Pinar del Río and Havana suffer the most, particularly on the south coast where wind-driven flood waves sweep destructively over the low coastline. Of the six provinces, Oriente and Pinar del Río are predominantly rural, Camagüey and Las Villas are marginally rural, while Havana and Matanzas give Cuba an overall urban majority. In 1953, fifty-seven per cent of the population lived in towns. Out of a total population of approximately seven million, more than one million live in La Habana and its suburb of Mariano. Santiago, with a hundred and eighty thousand, and Santa Clara trail a long way behind. Until the Revolution Cuba's wealth, services, talent, culture, and ambitions were unhealthily concentrated in Havana. So, too, were tourism and its cousin, vice.

Castro's policy has been to get Cuba out of Havana.

In Cuba Art and Revolution are close collaborators. Throughout the countryside one encounters huge posters which are striking in impact and original in design. The artists have managed to convey heroic euphoria without resorting to that jutting-jawed blockheadedness so characteristic of Soviet posters, with their Charles Atlas men and their Charles Atlas women, shirtsleeves rolled up and eyes lifted towards a permanently glowing horizon of production quotas surpassed. Though no judge of these matters, I conclude that the Cuban artists achieve their effects by heavy reliance on the woodcut and the etching, whose myriad of finely interwoven lines compel a greater attention to style and form.

'Guerrillas for Solidarity.' Rafael drives on, with Pedro dozing at his side. The traffic is sparse and only occasionally are we forced to slow down, usually for a tractor. We pass a farm called Lenin, then a large co-operative tractor station. In the middle of fields a huge housing estate suddenly sprouts —Carlos is immediately on his feet to explain that dwellings tend to be allocated after discussion, often heated, within a particular production unit, whether farm or factory. The aim of the architects, he says, is to break down these housing estates into humanly tolerable sub-units, each with its own day-nursery, shops, and services. We see infants frolicking in gaily coloured playgrounds.

In Matanzas, an important port, carnival masks are hanging from lamp-posts and fluorescent paper trailers are looped above the streets. But Rafael glances at his watch, shakes his head and, obviously a man enchanted by his profession, keeps his foot pressed down until we are out of the town and cutting southwards across the island, through the province of Las Villas, towards the port of Cienfuegos. In a small town called Colón, Rafael finally admits that others also have a right to work, and reluctantly passes the wheel to Pedro. Climbing out of the coach in search of soft drinks, we become the objects of a desultory scrutiny. Donkeys plod through the streets frightening the grunting old trucks; a small town in Latin America. Round a bar which manifestly has nothing to offer except water, a patient gathering of local people waits with Micawber-like optimism. Or maybe it's just a cool place to stand. Still thirsty, we resume our journey.

Nicole is sitting in front, beside Carlos. They talk for a while in Spanish, then Carlos falls asleep. Madame Bourgeois, carried she knows not where, is also asleep, her claws locked round her bulging white purse. Created by Balzac, she is a courageous old bag, passing seventy, staunch in the face of physical discomfort, and determined to taste every wine before her Maker finally knocks over her glass. She has toured the temples of Japan, climbed in the foothills of the Himalayas, and ransacked the boutiques of Singapore; she owns fourteen apartment houses in Paris, and she doesn't give a damn for anyone.

The Old Swiss sits by himself. This may be an act of free will (he ruminates), or it may be due to the fact that he hasn't yet changed his shirt. The Young Swiss, now recovered from his orgy of Coppelia ice-creams and, in his straw hat, twice the man he was, occasionally shuffles up the aisle of the coach to borrow cigarettes from Martha and to whisper in my ear that socialism is 'crap, man'. Immediately in front of us, Monsieur and Madame Lepinay, good Communists from Saint-Etienne, have nothing to say to each other. Spruce, bronzed, and rather younger in appearance than his wife, Monsieur Lepinay will gradually abandon himself to a terrible, consuming vice—love of the sun. Always the first to strip down to a fancy, flowered swimsuit, he will invariably be the last to tear himself away from any pool or beach where he can expose his flesh to the intoxicating socialist sun.

The port of Cienfuegos is named after the popular guerrilla leader, Camillo Cienfuegos, a comrade of Fidel and Che Guevara, who died mysteriously in a plane crash in 1959. (To their credit, the Cubans do not name streets or towns after leaders still living.) As our coach manoeuvres its passage with difficulty up a narrow, one-way street, its Soviet engine coughs at the effort, then dies. Pedro coaxes it, then Rafael intervenes with a master's touch: but to no avail. We are stranded fifty yards from our hotel. In Cuba there are no hotel porters; the elderly must either struggle with their own baggage or rely on the mercy of travelling companions. As for Rafael and Pedro, they are prepared to unload the suitcases from the bowels of the coach, but no more than that—not a yard further; and if these two charming idlers represent the real work ethic of Cuba, then one can consign all the beautiful posters to the museums.

I don't know what era the San Carlos Hotel belongs to, but it's the wrong one. Without air-conditioning and devoid of elevators, each flight of stairs is a staggered Everest leading to another flight. The rooms are small and pokey and dark and hot, to say the least. But, of course, there is a bar, and next to the bar a delicious, cool, empty room lined with chess tables. The pieces, in green and white, and made of a shiny, plastic-like substance which will withstand outbursts of rage, are drawn up in their deceptively passive rows, poised, waiting for the catalytic intervention of human intelligence. Carlos accepts my challenge before dinner; I make a couple of elementary errors and he does me the courtesy of tipping my king over on my behalf, to the discreet satisfaction of a crowd of Cuban Capablancas gathered to see the pale-skinned *inglés* turn even paler. Their restrained smiles are not easily forgotten during dinner, and I sulk. A group of professional musicians, much employed on the radio (Carlos says), slowly circumnavigate our long table, wailing peasant songs in the harsh, strident tone which reminds me of English medieval ballads.

In Cuba, to sing and to accompany oneself on the guitar is regarded as a manly attribute. The singer is often accompanied by a player of the *claves* (two hardwood sticks which clack) and of the *maracas* (gourds filled with seed or shot, which give the shuffle sound of calypso). The *punto guajira* is regarded as the authentic peasant music, and these days, with foreign and particularly American influences frowned on, most of what one hears is *guajira* music. But the juke-boxes which the Americans left behind are still prized and lovingly serviced, though Castro has called them 'imperialist jukeboxes'. The recordings I hear of 'Guantanamera' seem lifeless and thin compared with the one which used to enliven my grilled-steak lunches in New York five years ago.

The following morning is 'free'. It has to be: the Soviet engine will yield neither to reason nor emotion. A phone call has gone through to INIT, the national tourist agency, and something recuperative is expected to happen, as Rafael puts it, 'any time'. Seeing my gloomy expression, he slaps me on the back: 'Eming-way, *si*, Capablanca, *no*.' As we wander into the street I wonder when the news of my chess defeat will reach the pages of *Granma*. (Nevertheless, Mr Caute's visit greatly strengthens the political, economic, social, and cultural ties between the two peoples.)

Outside a restaurant a queue waits to eat. It is at least two hundred yards long and the citizens in the street who can see in through the windows are gazing enviously at their guzzling predecessors (who no doubt intend to stay there for ever). Though it is a working morning, the greater part of the male population of Cienfuegos has taken up strategic positions at the street corners, puffing cigars, chatting, observing, passing judgment. I suppose this massive masculine presence can be attributed to the shift system of work now favoured in Cuba: or is it the shiftless system?

The schoolchildren are on holiday. They are playing everywhere, in the streets, in the squares, in the small, grassless parks, well-dressed, clean, alert, playful, unafraid, and inquisitive. Only sit down for a moment and show a human face, and you are the Pied Piper. The little girls examine Martha's clothes, bracelet, ring, purse, shoes, hair, and eyelashes with bubbling curiosity—but also, and I stress this—with charming self-possession. The boys would like to have my Biro pen, cigarettes, chewing-gum, marbles, a new bicycle, and signed photographs of the Beatles.

Before the Revolution, Cuban illiteracy was at a lower level than in most Latin American countries. Even so, illiteracy ran as high as twenty-three per cent; among rural children sixty-one per cent did not attend school. The Castro régime made a priority of ending this situation. The first task was to solve the chronic shortage of teachers in the provinces. In thirty months, by converting military barracks into schools and by building new ones, the Government opened more classrooms than in the previous thirty years. Boarding schools were set up on confiscated estates and in Havana new 'peasant schools' (*escuelas campesinas*) were established in three hundred confiscated luxury houses. 1961 was officially declared the Year of Education. Secondary-school pupils took part in a massive campaign (perhaps on the Chinese model) to eliminate adult illiteracy; as a result, the secondary schools were closed for eight months. So great is Cuba's reliance on youth, on the new generation, that today a rural supervisor of twenty thousand schoolchildren may be only twenty years old, and it is not uncommon for pupils of fifteen or sixteen to begin part-time teaching.

Great emphasis was laid on the need to educate girls as well as boys. If Castro is to be believed, by 1962 fifty per cent of first-year medical students were females.

Here one must resort to statistics. In 1957 the national educational budget was 74 million pesos; in 1967 it was 333 millions. In ten years the régime increased the number of primary schools from 7,567 to 14,726, the number of pupils from 717,417 to 1,444,395, and the number of teachers from 17,355 to 47,876. In the secondary and high schools the teaching staff increased fourfold and the pupils almost tripled. In the technical and professional colleges the pupils increased from 6,259 to 29,975 and the teachers from 818 to 2,180. Before the Revolution Cuba had no agricultural colleges; ten years later there were thirty-seven, with 36,812 pupils. The régime has also established the first two fishery colleges.

Primary education, of course, is free. In October 1968 the number of scholarships available to all other levels was 244,718.

Since 1967, in an effort to increase the productive capacity of women, all infants attend nursery school from their forty-fifth day. To my mind, that is too early. Besides, there is another aspect. The rapid emancipation of women, of mothers, in Cuba and many other countries carries in practice the danger of an intensified exploitation of women. Male attitudes are slow to change; the woman who works all day finds that she must also do the shopping, feed the children, clean the house, and in most respects undertake the chores of the traditional mother. In time she becomes a recalcitrant heroine; one notes that more and more Soviet women are staying at home. The light just isn't worth the candle. I do not wish to be misunderstood. Far be it from me to argue that the woman's place is in the home; but it partly is and will remain so until the biological functions of motherhood are superseded; the conclusion must therefore be that a wife and mother can enter the world of labour to her own advantage only at the pace by which her menfolk are able to adjust generously to the displacement.

Certain educational theorists in Cuba are toying with the notion of almost universal boarding-school education (an idea far too expensive to implement as yet) and they, in my opinion, should be slapped across the head. If Cuba aspires to be Sparta, she will know some woes.

The slogans for Cuban children are: Study, Work, the Rifle. Work means that children over the age of six have to take part in productive labour at weekends and during the holidays. (Judging by the crowd of Biro-hunters gathered round me in the Cienfuegos square, these duties are less than all-consuming.) The emphasis is on physical fitness and learning by rote, on sculpting good patriots and good Communists. (An American may call this indoctrination, but his own children salute the flag in school and are assiduously protected from any textbook tainted by the faintest whiff of socialism.) Nor is Cuban education 'progressive' in any John Deweyite sense; as is invariably the case where the main task is to extend numeracy and literacy to children whose parents did not attend school, the teacher relies on 'A, B, C . . .', on multiplication tables, on discipline, on a uniform approach. And yet, at the secondary and higher levels, post-Revolutionary Cuban education perhaps has more in common with Dewey's teaching than did the old, traditionalist school, which relied on academic curricula to produce an élite solidly grounded in the humanities, literature, and rhetoric. Both Dewey and the new Cuban theories stress life-adjustment, practical know-how, and work orientation. Yet there is a crucial difference. Whereas Cuba is actively processing its students for pre-set productive roles on the basis of a planned economy, American education prides itself on offering to the individual a wide choice of subjects adapted to his or her private needs; and if the most urgent need is for a course in 'dating', so be it. Or home economics. But the Cubans have a long march to make before they can bring their civilization to such a pitch of flexibility.

We say goodbye to our children and set off to explore the streets of Cienfuegos. Once again I am trying to read people's faces, to find clues to questions only vaguely formulated. I can certainly confirm Andrew Salkey's observation that Cubans today lack a trace of that sullen, dispossessed look so familiar in Kingston and other West Indian towns where neo-colonialism has replaced direct rule.

One never encounters dumb insolence, self-pitying shrugs and grimaces, peevish nonsense, sudden hysteria. The foreign visitor is neither envied nor resented; there is confidence that his ultimate verdict will be favourable, that he will see the light. There still prevails an implicit sense of the first person plural rarely to be found, in my experience, among the Communist countries of Eastern Europe. Almost every Cuban regards himself as Fidel's *compañero*, whereas in Eastern Europe it is 'they', the bosses, who capriciously regulate the lives of a 'we', whose unity does not extend beyond the commonality of our predicament, our powerlessness. How long the Cuban spirit of solidarity, of collective pride, will last I cannot know. One must admit that it is cemented not only by the ever-present threat from a formidable enemy, but also by a romantic, even childish susceptibility to heroic myth. Thus a typical Cuban feels himself to have stormed the Moncada Barracks at Fidel's side, to have waded ashore from the *Granma*, to have endured the hardships of the Sierra Maestra, to have entered Havana in triumph, and to have personally conquered the *marabu*, the fast-spreading, thorny parasite which is the great enemy of agriculture.

On this particular day the mood of 'we-ness' gains added colour from a festivity of flags and portraits celebrating the rising of September 1957, when Batista's Air Force boss, Tabernilla, retaliated by massacring over one thousand people. Here the Cuban spirit is perhaps more familiar to an American than to an Englishman; both Americans and Cubans miss no opportunity to commemorate epoch-making events in their history with national holidays and ostentatious displays of patriotic devotion, whereas the British rather tamely calendar their days-off as 'Bank Holidays' and convoy patiently towards the sea without a thought for Magna Carta or Charles's head, and without a single Union Jack to hoist over their caravans. Privileged inhabitants of

God's little smoke-choked acre, they take it all for granted and leave the countryside littered with empty bottles.

After lunch we gather for a special treat—a boat trip from the inner harbour to the sea. Our Soviet coach still stubbornly impervious to its duty, a dapper mini-bus, perhaps of Italian origin, carries us swiftly to the waiting boat. A light, warm breeze fans our faces as we chug gently through the succession of widening bays which form the barrier between the harbour and the violent storms to which this stretch of coastline is prey. Beer bottles rattle in the icebox and pretty soon the spirit on board is more than comradely, with Rafael and Carlos in operatic mood and cormorants skimming across the water. Rafael, bottle in hand, cha-chas across the deck, swaying his hips enticingly in front of Madame Bourgeois, who, having failed to locate a boutique on board, merely nods. (She has seen it all in *gai Paris*.) During a lull in the concert, the Young Swiss decides to show us what it's really about and begins to yodel. The company is hushed, awe-struck; Rafael's expression is that of a man confronted by the supernatural. The yodel pierces the placid waters, fish leap ecstatically, birds take flight from the exotic trees which rim the bay, little rowing boats wobble at their moorings, and the stilts supporting the fishermen's huts collapse. A large Soviet cargo-ship, on an urgent mission to collect sugar, turns rapidly about and flees back to Odessa.

At the end of it all only the Young Swiss remains unaffected. He blinks, adjusts his hat, borrows one of my cigarettes, and confides to me that he has wind of 'a hole' further down the island where cigarettes are 'dirt cheap, dig that'. How the sea heals the soul of man! Sunlight dancing on the waves, fishermen's nets hanging out to dry, beach cabins nestling on strips of golden sand. But the fair-skinned had better look out. Ominous blotches of red have appeared on exposed expanses of neck, shoulder, and arm. Tubes of protective cream change hands.

On our return, the afternoon is still young and we make tracks for the Hotel Jagua, once a preserve of the rich, but now occupied by ordinary Cuban families on vacation. We, the Western bourgeoisie, gape in envy as we wander through the elegant lounges, peep into a huge George Raft bar furnished in red and black mock-leather from which daylight is rigorously excluded (no self-respecting Cuban bar has a window), gaze into the swish hairdressing salon and examine the bookstalls. A translation of G. M. Trevelyan's history of the English Revolution of 1688, bearing a red flag on the cover, catches my eye. Now it is time to plunge into the swimming-pool, or rather leap, because the paving stones which surround it to a width of six feet are too hot for the feet to tolerate even momentarily. The pool is small, deliciously warm, and heavily populated. I notice that whereas in England anyone brave enough to enter a chilly open-air pool immediately swims like a desperate puppy for the few frantic moments before cramp sets in, here, as in many hot climates, people wallow like seals, gurgling gently, soothing away the months of toil.

The Jagua, we all agree, is a great improvement on the San Carlos! But it is to the mountaineer's slopes of the San Carlos that we, underprivileged foreigners, must now withdraw. On arrival we find that our bathroom is without water of any temperature; on this occasion my plumber's skills are unavailing. The evening meal is mediocre and the absence of fruit seems particularly galling. One expects this deprivation in Russia, East Germany, or Czechoslovakia, but not in tropical Cuba. I ask Nicole what has happened to the citrus fruit. She braces herself for battle.

'How do you imagine Cuba pays for the machinery she imports from the socialist countries?'

I challenge Carlos to a game of chess but he prefers for the time being to savour his victory. Bored to death, Martha and I return to our room and play a game on our pocket set.

Still no water. Thunder is heard out to sea. We lather ourselves in anti-mosquito cream and fall asleep, happy to be together.

The next day begins with a visit to the Cienfuegos sugar-exporting plant, Cuba's largest, a huge concrete silo with a rail yard at one end and shoots dipping down to the pier at the other. (Sugar cane is perennial but its yield decreases yearly, so that by the sixth year the yield is only a fifth of the first season's. Fields are generally then resown. Usually the harvest, or zafra, occurs during the one hundred days of winter beginning in November, when the sugar content of the cane is at its peak.) Traditionally, of course, Cuba depended on the quota, an American commitment to buy a guaranteed tonnage at a price normally two cents per pound above the world market-price. This arrangement certainly improved Cuba's terms of trade in the 1950s, but the bargain also spelled dependence; about forty per cent of Cuban sugar production rested in American hands, and the United States, moreover, expected Cuba to grant her in return a preferential import tariff. But the worst aspect of it, so Castro and Guevara believed, was that it tied Cuba to a single-crop economy, forcing her to mark time while other nations industrialized, and so putting her perpetually at the mercy of fluctuating world prices. In March 1960 Guevara, then president of the National Bank, described the quota as 'economic slavery', and in July the United States refused to renew it. Immediately the Soviet Union stepped in and Khrushchev committed her to buy Cuba's sugar surplus.

In those early days the golden word among Cuban economists was 'diversification', which in turn implied greater self-sufficiency and greater flexibility. But diversification did not work out well and gradually Castro's thinking came full circle until, in 1969-70, he launched a massive national effort to raise the zafra to ten million tons. (Six million was the norm.) Meanwhile, Cuba depended on

99

Russia's willingness to buy five million tons at six cents per pound. The Russian connection did not always work well: the new cane-cutting machines sent from the USSR merely damaged the cane. (Cane does not grow straight like maize or rice. When the sugar content is high it lies down; at harvest time it must be lifted, stripped of its leaves and cut in a certain way. Otherwise the next year's crop suffers.)

1969-70 was the year of sugar mania. Thousands of 'volunteers' were pulled from other work, the actual crop did not exceed eight and a half million tons, and the Cuban economy was wrecked, as Castro himself conceded in a remarkable *mea culpa* delivered in July 1970. But, as with Nasser after the Six Day War, defeat only reinforced popular loyalty (who else? who else?) and Castro's power survived unimpaired.

Inside the silo the brown sugar is piled in large, sweet-smelling mounds. The manager of the plant proudly shows us a conveyor-belt made in Russia and another made in France. He stresses that he would like to trade with us all, and that anyone can buy Cuban sugar, even Franco's Spain (which has also developed splendid commercial relations with Russia and China, idealists please note). I ask him whether he considers the old quota system with the United States to have been slavery. He says yes, definitely. I ask him why. Because, my friend, it bound Cuba to a single-crop economy. Yes, quite so, but surely not more so than when in 1970 the whole Cuban work force was delivered over to the *zafra*. The manager's tone is now slightly less relaxed. He very well appreciates that in certain foreign circles Cuba's failures cause great rejoicing. No, no, I am not rejoicing, merely trying to understand. The manager then asks me whether in Britain we do not make mistakes; are the rumours he hears of a bad balance of trade incorrect, and is he entirely wrong in believing that strikes are a great problem?

Our French contingent, and particularly Nicole, now

assume the gloating expectancy of ringside spectators awaiting the knock-out.

'The British balance of trade,' I say, 'is bad. The standard
of living is now one of the lowest in Western Europe. The
working class is constantly being urged to tighten its belt,
but declines to do so, well knowing that the preachers continue to fatten themselves.'

A small silence.

'In that case,' says Madame Lepinay, 'you are in no position to criticize Cuba.'

'Besides,' adds Monsieur Lepinay, 'there are no strikes in
Cuba.'

'That is because the trade unions are state-controlled.'

'The Cuban workers have the right to strike,' the manager
insists.

'Yes, that's so,' Carlos adds.

'In a socialist system,' Nicole says, 'the workers realize
that when they strike they strike against themselves.'

The French contingent are enthusiastic about this
formula: how logical, how true! I must attempt an answer:

'That is precisely what the British capitalists tell their
workers: higher wages mean inflated prices mean loss of
exports means unemployment. Disrupted assembly lines
mean loss of foreign orders means closures mean even more
unemployment. Don't cut your own throats!'

No, no, no: I have failed to understand the elementary
difference between capitalism and socialism. Under
capitalism, the worker is exploited and hoodwinked.

'Yes, certainly. But so he may be under socialism.'

No, no, impossible.

'Well, consider the events at Gdansk, which brought down
Gomulka. The Polish workers themselves did not fix rising
prices and they did not fix static wages. So they rebelled.
And the police beat them over the head, calling them foreign
spies.'

This gives cause for reflection.

'In Poland, there were mistakes,' says Monsieur Lepinay. 'These have now been rectified.'

'Only because the workers withdrew their labour and rioted.'

'I can see,' said the manager, 'that you will not be happy until the workers here in Cuba go on strike and riot. That will confirm your prejudices. Then the *gusanos* in Miami can return and give us the kind of economy you admire—an economy of perpetual strikes.'

An outbreak of clapping. Another bourgeois bites the dust.

I raise my voice slightly. 'The only point I want to make is this: a nationalized economy, like Cuba's, is not a workers' economy. Managers and administrators, like yourself, make all the crucial decisions, you mobilize labour, direct labour, discipline labour, and all the time you tell the workers that this silo belongs to them. You have a machinery for the ventilation of certain minor grievances, but that is all. You make absolutely sure that the trade unions can never challenge your power, your authority, but, on the contrary, act as transmission belts for your directives. I am not in a position to know whether things could be otherwise in Cuba. But, as the great Sartre once said, it is best to call a cat a cat.'

The manager politely glances at his watch and Nicole announces that we are all sabotaging the production effort. Monsieur Lepinay, who is in fact a very keen student of world affairs, now engages me in private conversation and, though our positions diverge, I feel pleased to have encountered a mind capable of transcending glib clichés and comfortable formulas.

In the first instance, the Cuban proletariat regarded Fidel Castro with some suspicion, if only because under Batista it enjoyed a relatively privileged position, union protection, and high wages. The old trade-union leaders were snuffed out by the Revolution and the last free election within the unions took place in 1961. In 1962 two major strikes occurred. In an interview, Guevara defended the strike as an ultimate weapon even under a socialist régime, but this outlook had few subscribers among the new men who took control of the unions.

Interesting evidence was provided by Maurice Zeitlin who, with Guevara's blessing, visited twenty-one plants in the six provinces during the summer of 1962. Seventy-three per cent of male workers fully endorsed the Revolution, but only sixty-two per cent of the female workers, twenty-five per cent of whom expressed active hostility. Workers unemployed or underemployed before the Revolution voiced a corresponding gratitude to it. Out of a sample of a hundred and forty-seven workers, forty-three per cent agreed that the Revolution had inspired in them a much more positive attitude to work, most of them explaining this in terms of wellbeing, dignity, and economic security. Only a few—and this is significant—offered answers which would delight Marxist students of capitalist 'alienation':

A: 'I sacrificed a part of my youth to learn my trade, and it is only now that I am working for myself—since the foreign enterprises passed into the hands of the Revolution.' B: 'I work freely now. It is as if I am my own boss.' C: 'Before, I worked for another individual or for a company. Now I work for the people, that is, to provide hospitals, houses, etc., and whatever else the country needs.'

However time-serving the spirit behind this last pat testimony, it contains a good deal of truth. But the previous respondent is also interesting: 'It is as if I am my own boss.' Much hinges on that 'as if'. Unfortunately our visit to the sugar silo does not culminate in a field investigation of our own; during the entire hour not a single worker comes into view. The shift system, no doubt.

In the interval before lunch we settle down in the lobby to watch television in the company of many interested spectators who have drifted in from the street. The Cubans are a highly televisual people. At the time of the Revolution there were four hundred thousand sets. Today one finds public sets in side-streets, heavily protected and supported by concrete stands. Fidel's own success as *el jefe máximo* owes much to his oratorical skills and to his mastery of the marathon TV discourse. During our visit we happen to see him only once on the box—he has driven to the airport in his green fatigues to receive a delegation of stolid, square, regular, double-breasted bureaucrats from Eastern Europe. Then they drive through Havana in open cars, waving to the schoolgirls. I cannot really judge the overall quality of Cuban television apart from the almost universally poor reception. A stark, formalistic ballet of Carmen proves enjoyable and visually original, but otherwise the Cubans seem to get dreary rubbish where we get lively rubbish.

The main passion of the moment is the Munich Olympic Games, but the coverage is technically appalling, being for the most part confined to 'stills' of Soviet giants lifting ever heavier weights. A movie-medium certainly suffers when it doesn't move. Generally Soviet and East German successes are loudly celebrated, as are North American disasters and disappointments. Four pretty Cuban girls (all black) win a gold medal in the 4 x 100 metres relay and every Cuban feels he helped to carry the baton. But real ecstasy is reserved for the utterly cathartic victory of the Cuban heavy-weight boxing champion, Stevenson (yes), over his American rival. (In this context I pick two pleasing phrases out of *Granma:* '*el peso completo*', meaning the heavyweight category, and '*horizontalazó al norteamericano*', which encourages a literal rather than an idiomatic translation: Stevenson 'horizontalized the North American'!) Bravo and, what is more, Stevenson immediately reveals socialist virtue by proudly refusing the pleas of American promoters to turn professional. Blood in your nose, mud in your eye.

These days the Communist states regard sporting achievements as symbols of national prestige and national health, and I notice that we turn sour on the idea when they snatch all the medals. Even so, passionate addict of sport that I am, I am inclined to adapt the famous epigram: happy is the land that needs no heroes of sport. Just as romantic film stars primarily satisfy the needs of adolescents and others starved of private sexual love, so the most hysterical soccer crowds are mainly composed of frustrated young men who live in cities too mean to provide them with football fields of their own. Travelling by the London underground, I observe long lines of my fellow-countrymen too short of breath to climb the moving escalator yet eagerly reading about a handful of crazy Britons grappling with the summit of Everest. America is both the land of the sports scholarship and of the over-fed man knocked out by a coronary at the age of fifty. The general disinclination of young Frenchwomen to spend their youth grinding round a cinder track in pursuit of stronger legs than some rival from the Ukraine strikes me as profoundly rational.

It's farewell to Cienfuegos. At least it looks so until our Soviet engine, after an initial roar of great pride, sounding like a bull suddenly let loose in a field of cows, dies. More phone calls. Madame Bourgeois sits on her suitcase in the shade, guarding her many little gifts. The Old Swiss, still in the same shirt, expresses loud disgust and offers to mend the engine himself. Nicole's strained expression seems to say, 'such things can happen anywhere', while Carlos sinks into complete apathy. The Young Swiss strides up and down the street in his straw hat, talking insanely about private enterprise. Martha finds a corner and buries herself in Flaubert.

A roar! A cheer! Diesel fumes choke the narrow street, but no one seems to mind, for every machine is a triumph of progress and, like a man successful with women, entitled to boast a bit.

The trip to Trinidad takes us through the Sierra d'Escambray, with a stop-off at a lush botanical garden in the countryside, where we lose ourselves in a haze of delicious scents and strong colours. I abandon the attempt to think and deliver my soul, like Alice, to visions of an underground world where every rule is irregular. In Oxford Street I had dreamed of Revolutionary Cuba, and here, somewhere in the province of Las Villas, soothed by little waterfalls, pink flowers, and blue-crested birds, I dream myself so rich that I need never work again nor write another word.

When we reach Trinidad I am asleep and don't wish to know about it, but a glimpse out of the window revealing car-less cobbled streets and mobs of ragged urchins wakes me up. This little town, the oldest in Cuba, founded in 1514, was liberated by Che Guevara himself, but did not want to be liberated, being both Catholic and conservative, and henceforward became a favourite haunt of counter-revolutionaries in hiding. Every house is a little church, hushed and solemn, with peeping eyes, and through the grilled windows one sees shrines and crucifixes and rosaries and pictures of the Sacred Heart. In Cuba religious worship is still tolerated, but the roots have been cut and all the religious schools have been closed. Few children are baptized, and marriages in church are rare. In fact, the Church was not very influential in Cuba even before the Revolution, with only one priest for every nine or ten thousand inhabitants— a population more superstitious than faithful. But what Castro calls 'any good Catholic, a sincere Catholic ... who supports the Revolution, who is against imperialism ...' will not be persecuted. We enter the main church of Trinidad and just inside the door I find a chart depicting the duties of good Catholics who are called, ironically, 'militantes'. Carlos agrees to laugh about this but Trinidad makes him shake his head in sorrow.

Cutting inland, we stop briefly at the old town of Sancti

Spiritus, also liberated by Che. Then, moving east, we pass into the province of Camagüey, the great cattle ranch of Cuba, flat and lush and strewn with galloping cowboys. It was here that a prize bull costing $100,000 was imported from Canada and set about its happy work of blending strains. (But it is the climate as well as the poor strains which make the cattle of Camagüey so unproductive in American or European terms, and which creates acute shortages of meat, butter, and milk.) The coach sweeps past a series of clean, orderly, white-painted milking and cattle stations, some bearing the names of Communist saints. Martha, lulled by the hum of the tyres on the tarmac, falls asleep on my shoulder.

Outside the city of Camagüey we stop to inspect a new institute for training cattle-experts. Such institutions did not exist before the Revolution. Cuba's rural workers, or seventy per cent of them, worked on the great estates, or *latifundia*, for private landowners (eight per cent of whom owned over seventy per cent of cultivated land). The children of the two hundred thousand peasant families, and of the hundred and forty thousand poor renters or squatters, grew up illiterate and without hope. And so also did those of the six hundred thousand rural proletarians, mainly cane-cutters, who found employment only during the harvest. These children would die where they were born, and none the wiser. More than seventy-five per cent of them lived in *bohios*, huts made out of royal palm tree, with roofs of leaves and floors of earth. Others, the children of *desalojos*, or homeless squatters evicted from the *latifundia*, lived in cribs along the side of a road. The per caput income of the peasantry was less than one-third of the national average. Not that all urban dwellers were fortunate, for many thousands in Havana, for example, lived in *solares*, or alleys lined with one-room dwellings in which the poor huddled a dozen to the room, tucked away discreetly in the well-off neighbourhoods to provide cheap domestic service. A *solar* of two hundred or more people could rarely boast of more than two toilets.

In those days there was a theoretical minimum wage: seventy-five dollars a month. But only sixty per cent of the working population earned so much. It is true that more people had been brought into the money economy than anywhere else in Latin America, but that only made the majority conscious of where the money was going. Besides, the classic recipe for revolution is gross inequality plus a rising standard of living.

We amble about the half-built institute, among the piles of sand, unlaid pipes, cement-mixers, and tip-trucks. The construction workers are sitting in the shade drinking from flasks. Not a machine is working, not a girder rising, not a hammer hammering—the shift system. The dormitory and refectory are already built, and a certain number of students have taken up residence. The dormitory consists of two-tier bunks in rows so close as to suggest a concentration camp, and the base of the beds is made from sugar-cane wood. Nevertheless, resources are scarce, students need not be coddled, and something is moving.

'What do you think?' Carlos asks me.

'Excellent. When do the construction workers begin work again?'

He looks puzzled.

Compared with Cienfuegos, Camagüey is a hive of activity, a bustle. The streets of the old town are packed with beauty salons, shoe shops, barber shops, and, of course, people standing about. Here, in the evening, the young males roam like hungry wolves, intense, brash, quick-tongued, and quite prepared to follow and proposition a single foreign girl. (We carry a few in our group.) But they lack the demonic persistence of the predatory Italian. Passing a small radio station—Radio Liberación—and a large poster bearing the portrait of Ho Chi Minh and words indicating solidarity with bombed Haiphong, we return to the Hotel Gran where the delinquent water system finally yields to my expertise.

The next day we visit the headquarters of the Young Pioneers situated in a pleasant, gardened house, previously a brothel. A sweet little girl in a uniform greets us with a salute and a speech lasting four seconds. The girls wear blue and white cravats and upstairs they have a glass case full of the cravats of all the Young Pioneers of the whole world. The house is spotless; in the entrance hall hangs a huge and lurid portrait of Che. Carlos tells me that Pioneers are boys and girls, aged seven to twelve, who join the movement only if their parents consent. (Some Catholic parents refuse, since the teaching is strictly Marxist-Leninist.)

The kids are divided into groups of twenty, according to their interests, and then set to work in rooms lined with maps, pictures, and charts, with globes, model tractors, model fishing-fleets, blackboards, plants, soil-samples, mineral specimens, knitting needles, and old cotton-reels (God's finest gift to any inventive child). The hallway upstairs is lined with photos of Cubans and Bolivians who fought along-side Che in Bolivia. A glass case displays glossy photos of blond Soviet Pioneers rapturously marching, hiking, camp-ing, sailing, and generally setting an example. Slightly more incongruous are snapshots of Soviet soldiers entering a defeated and destroyed Berlin in 1945. That, somehow, seems far away and long ago.

The little girls serve us glasses of orange juice, look shy, and wave goodbye to us. What a load of freaks we must look!

The museum at Camagüey is full of interesting things. A huge mural, for example, drawn in black ink, depicts in loving detail and with delicate lines the history of Cuba from Columbus to Castro. A worthy female guide, one of those solemn, monotonous exemplars of social rectitude, takes us round the Natural History section leaving no stone, fish, or spider unturned, but things liven up when Carlos threatens to have me put in a pair of iron slave-manacles unless I abandon my revisionist heresies, and Rafael intervenes to plead that I am 'a good fell-ow' and generally 'Eming-way'. Item: a series of lively wall-cartoons depicting the puppet leaders of Cuba since 1902, notably Grau San Martín, Machado, and Batista. Item: a wooden cabinet from colonial days in which drinking water was filtered through a stone bowl. Item: a varied exhibition of paintings carrying the prefatory notice that some Cuban artists have managed to endow new formal developments with a revolutionary content.

As our party disintegrates, wandering in all directions, Martha and I are nervously approached by a gentleman who turns out to be the Director of the Museum. The soul of courtesy, he invites us into his office and proudly takes down from his shelves catalogues in Spanish put out by the Tate and National Galleries in London.

'How I would like to see all these masterpieces for myself,' he says.

'Could you not make the journey?'

He smiles sadly. 'Our budget does not run to it.'

I congratulate him on his collection of Cuban paintings and mention that, in my opinion, it will be a sad day for Cuba if socialist realism ever becomes the only accepted aesthetic in the fine arts.

'There is no danger of that,' he says decisively. 'We must tread our own path of development.'

'It has already happened in literature.'

He offers a small gesture. 'No doubt you have your own opinion about that.'

Martha mentions that we are most anxious to buy one or two lithographs or etchings by contemporary Cuban artists. Does the museum have any for sale?

'Unfortunately not. For that you must go to a gallery.'

Could he please recommend us a good gallery in Havana?

'Well, just a moment, please.' He begins to take down directories from a shelf. He searches, mutters, licks his thumb to turn the pages, scratches his head. Finally, he writes down the names of two galleries.

'But I am not sure,' he says. 'It is a long time since I was in Havana.'

We thank him and rise to leave, but he indicates that he would like us to stay. He is a shy old gentleman and, I would guess, a very learned one, devoted to his museum and to the cultural life of Camagüey. He wants us to sit with him not only because we have shown a polite appreciation, but also because he feels cut off from a wider world of which we, in a transitory sense, are ambassadors. At that instant I see in him—and this is pure speculation—a noble but rather sad example of self-sacrifice. So many of his colleagues and peers departed, but he remained, hopeful perhaps, patriotic perhaps, anxious to serve, to be of some value to his emergent people. And here he is now, still at his desk late at night, isolated, thumbing catalogues from a great metropolis five thousand miles away, striving in the silence to connect.

We shake his hand. 'Come back soon,' he says.

Our stay in Cienfuegos was too long, in Camagüey too brief. Once again we sweep across this flat land of cattle and horses, of cowboys, empty swimming-pools, and dead motor cars, past fields of coffee (a small plant growing close to the ground), of mango, paw-paw, and cucumber. As we pass slow-moving trucks groaning with their load of workers we wave and are waved to in a continuous process of mutual salutation which is as pleasing as it is meaningless.

For lunch we stop at a country club once exclusive to the rich. The food is excellent and the big swimming-pool has no water. Monsieur Lepinay, stripped down in a trice to his flowered bathing trunks, is appalled by this sacrilege. He delivers a speech about it and Carlos looks sad. Then, making the best of a bad job, Monsieur Lepinay hurls himself upon the grass, stretches out like a pinned wrestler with his face turned up to the divine sun, and soaks. Presently the Young Swiss emerges from behind a bush, wearing his straw hat and a pair of bathing trunks. Having discarded his spectacles he is short-sighted, and Carlos dares him to take a running jump into the deep end of the pool. Sensing that the honour of capitalism, Switzerland, and American Express is at stake, and emitting a piercing yodel, the Young Swiss breaks into a gallop. Rafael is doubled up with laughter. The Old Swiss is staring aghast. Nicole screams, and the other women release warning yells. The Young Swiss stops just in time, hovering on the brink of the empty pool. He turns, flushed and blinking. The women scold Carlos, who looks sheepish.

Standing at the open-air bar, I am about to hand over a ten-peso note when I see that it bears the signature 'Che', denoting the time when Guevara, that passionate opponent of money, was president of the National Bank. I hesitate. Such notes are now rare and Martha thinks I should keep it, or she should. But where would we put it? Would we show it to guests after dinner until everyone stayed away? It then strikes me that, maybe in ten years' time, maybe in fifteen, we could have it auctioned at Sotheby's in London and collect a fat dividend. Disgusted by this train of thought I give it to the barman. Immediately he spots Che's signature and puts it aside.

Che. Magic name, noble man, romantic legend—the asthmatic who flogged and mortified his own flesh for an ideal. Che. In Cuba today he is a Christ, crucified by the combined efforts of the Bolivian Communist Party (the Pharisees) and the CIA (Pilate). And not only in Cuba: wherever young hearts beat with the quickened tempo of revolt, you will find his poster-portrait pinned to the peeling wall, eyes uplifted, the beret framing his head like a halo, locks of hair curling down his neck. Even in his lifetime this Argentinian doctor was a legend, a Garibaldi, and constantly reported to have died in the Congo, in Vietnam, in Latin America. The Central Intelligence Agency and the Pentagon's counter-insurgency experts read his notes on *Guerrilla Warfare* and took elaborate notes of their own—to combat Satan, study his Bible. For them, masters of 'pacification', stonemasons of 'stability', Che was a roving barrel of dynamite, a migrant asp, hiding, stinging, hiding again. We offer any reward for this man's head!

To what extent he was a victim of his own legend I am not competent to judge. But, having read his *Reminiscences of the Cuban War* and his *Bolivian Diary*, I doubt it. He never took the easy path; he never believed that rhetoric, fine sentiments, and brave postures alone could make a revolution (or a genuine revolutionist). He was a patient, persevering technician of social formations and guerrilla strategy, largely self-taught (experience was his school, though he read avariciously) and highly self-critical. It is a mistake to think of him as an orthodox Communist or an agent of Moscow. On the contrary, he had nothing but contempt for the urban-based, compromising, reformist, Moscow-led Communist Parties of Latin America.

What is more, he possessed an attractive quality rare in orthodox Communists. He was happier out of power than in. His role as Cuban Minister for Industries was, as he later openly confessed, marred by mistakes, notably the reckless importation of new factories from Russia and Eastern Europe. But it was not these mistakes which led him, in 1965, to abandon power, office, and comfortable prestige in pursuit of desperate adventures, a renewed gamble with his life, this time fatal. He had always made it clear to Castro that he would not stay for long, that his mission extended to the whole of Latin America. When news of his death came,

Cuba was shaken; an era had ended, the enemy had learned the lesson.

Put simply, what Guevara dedicated his life to was the liberation of the peasant masses, their political, social, and economic emancipation. But these are fine phrases. Doubts persist in lingering. I do not refer to the feasibility of the project, but to its motivation. Those who, like Che, live by the gun, deserve close attention. There is a quality we call fanaticism when exhibited by our opponents and self-sacrifice by our allies. (Read any war story to confirm this.) After the Missile Crisis of 1962, Guevara wrote an article which was published only posthumously, six years later. In it he wrote: '... we proceed along the path of liberation even if this costs millions of atomic victims ...' Those of us who have always scorned the logic, the priorities, implicit in the phrase 'better dead than Red' are obliged, I think, to feel distinctly uneasy about a doctrine which can contemplate sacrificing the whole of one generation (a certain evil) for the benefit of a future one (an uncertain blessing). Two words are worth isolating: 'We proceed'. We proceed along the path of liberation even if ... WE proceed. One is entitled to distrust all such WEs.

Washington, however, did not fear Che because he knew how to sling a hammock between trees or because he was a hard man to ambush; he was feared because he was an uncompromising enemy of private property and because he had played a prime role in socializing the Cuban economy at the double.

It has to be remembered that when in January 1959 Guevara entered Havana a few days ahead of Castro, few Cubans and even fewer Americans had any clear idea of the economic doctrines of the 26 July Movement. There had been manifestoes inveighing against social injustice and foreign domination, but such diatribes constituted a routine part of any rebel programme in Cuba and few people took them seriously. 'Realities', common sense, and a little judicious pressure would surely work their customary miracle. Throughout the two years in the Sierra Maestra, Castro had in no way displayed affection for socialism. On the contrary, in an interview published in *Coronet* magazine in February 1958, he denigrated nationalization as 'at best, a cumbersome instrument' which would hinder speedy industrialization. Three months later he told Jules Dubois: 'Never has the 26 July Movement talked about socializing or nationalizing the industries.'

Within days of taking power the new régime won mass popularity by drastically cutting house rents for those below a certain income level. Empty building-sites were sold compulsorily. New wage agreements resulted in a fifteen per cent rise in real wages. Ominous? Maybe, and maybe not. This was traditional distributive politics, not socialism, and though the urban landlords might wince, the bourgeoisie as a whole might agree that some such gesture was an inevitable concession to popular expectations.

But the young rebels were frantically at work in the toolshed and in May the axe bit into the bark. The Land Reform decree, mainly drafted by Guevara's disciple Núñez Jimenez, a Marxist geographer and economist, abolished private estates of more than one thousand acres (except those with an exceptionally productive yield), distributed land to peasant families in holdings of sixty-seven acres (first claim going to sharecroppers), and set up co-operatives to be run by the Institute of Agrarian Reform (INRA). It was also announced that henceforward all sugar plantations must reside in Cuban hands.

Neither the Russians nor the Chinese had run nearly so fast. Panic and fury shook Cuba. Landowners held protest rallies and even hunger strikes. At this stage they had access to radio and television as well as to conservative newspapers like the *Diario de la Marina*, to attack the new law. The heartland of resistance was Camagüey, where the cattle-ranch owners were in a state of ferment. To the north, also, the Big Man stirred. A week after the Reform Law was promulgated, the United States Government despatched a formal note of protest and five members of the Cuban cabinet promptly resigned. This was interesting in two respects: first, these politicians weren't socialists; secondly, they shared the almost universal assumption that Cuba could not survive in the face of American hostility. And this helps to explain, I think, why the juvenile rebels hurried so far so fast; they were determined to cut the knot, and they knew that hesitation would merely bind them in impotence. In Ibsen's *A Doll's House*, the wife Nora puts on her topcoat and shoes *before* her final confrontation with her husband, knowing that if she does not she will remain in his house for ever.

Washington called for 'prompt, adequate, and effective compensation'. Cuba offered bonds in Cuban currency, maturing in twenty years at an annual interest of four and a half per cent. Not a very big deal. And how would the expropriated lands be assessed? Here the chickens came home to roost. Castro announced that he would accept the valuations which the landowners and corporations them-selves had filed with the Batista or Castro Governments. But, of course, the owners had deliberately undervalued their properties to evade taxes.

Cuba and the United States were now headed on a collision course.

After the 1960 sugar harvest, two million seven hundred thousand acres belonging to the sugar mills were expropri-ated, and one thousand co-operatives were created. United Fruit claimed that it had lost eighty million dollars' worth of land, but the Cubans divided that estimate by five. In June, the refineries of Esso, Shell, and Texaco were taken over after the companies had refused to process Soviet oil. In

October, INRA took over three hundred and eighty-two large enterprises, including one hundred and sixty-six belonging to American companies. The second Urban Reform Law limited each individual to one residence. On 1 May 1961 Castro announced a 'socialist Cuba'. Within the space of two years all the major economic enterprises, all the instruments of education and public information, all the labour unions and professional associations, had been nationalized. Socialism, or Communism, had come to the Caribbean. In addition, INRA had supervised the reclamation of four hundred and forty thousand acres of scrub land, which had been planted with rice, cotton, and potatoes, virtually ending the bane and distress of the old system, rural unemployment.

But all was not well. The economy was spiralling into chaos and confusion, wrecked by the haphazard decisions of an inexperienced bureaucracy. Both Castro and Guevara readily admitted to a catastrophic history of errors. Russia had to bale Cuba out, but the Russians were complaining that Cuba was moving too fast. In 1962 mass demonstrations against lowered living standards took place at Cárdenas, El Cano, and Santa Clara, and were rigorously suppressed, with confiscations.

In 1963, the second Agrarian Reform restricted private estates to about one hundred acres (five *caballeriás*). As a result, some extremely productive farms were snuffed out. The co-operatives which replaced them were really state farms, devoid of genuine autonomy and subject to centralized direction from INRA. However, there still remain in Cuba between a hundred and fifty and two hundred thousand small independent farmers who grow seventy per cent of the fruit, ninety per cent of the coffee and tobacco, twenty-five per cent of the sugar, and who handle half the livestock. In principle they are obliged to market their produce through the State purchasing agency, but in practice a lively black market begins behind the private farmer's barn.

Their urban counterparts fared, in the long run, less well. In 1968 a new, pulverizing 'revolutionary offensive' closed down, without compensation, many small businesses from bars and restaurants to fruit-sellers. And this, as we have seen, scarcely infuses life or gaiety into the streets of Havana.

CHAPTER

4

Oriente

We now enter the easternmost and largest province of Cuba, Oriente. It was here that Castro and his eighty-one companions landed from the *Granma* in December 1956, the surviving remnants taking to the great mountain range known as the Sierra Maestra, from the southern peaks of which, on a clear day, one can see the coastline of Jamaica.

Oriente was, and still is, a province of poor peasants living in small, makeshift dwellings of palm wood, thatch, and leaves. They work in the sugar fields, among the tall banana plants with their large, dark green leaves, and they grow coconuts. But nowadays their little gardens are meticulously tended, they have laid neat, stone-paved pathways, they are adequately fed and healthy, their children go to school, and their innate dignity no longer has to compete with squalor. It's a world come to life, crowded with mobile workers, tractor and truck stations, long lines of painted excavators drawn up in neat rows, music and muzak blaring at every turn, men with cigars in their mouths and calm, inquisitive eyes. Faces which are neither aggressive nor obsequious; faces which belong to themselves.

Here and there one sees soldiers on guard, protecting a camp or some other installation, and everywhere little white schools have mushroomed, with those inevitable plaster busts of José Martí standing guard at the gate. Outside a farm, a plaque to Lenin; outside another, a hammer and sickle; outside a third, a huge placard: 'To Die for the Fatherland is to Live.' I ask Carlos about this: is there not some virtue in literal truth—to die for the fatherland is to die, and perhaps to be remembered?

He smiles (the Englishman is restless again). 'Quite so. To be remembered, to be honoured, is to live.'

Without doubt, death is as much a romantic obsession in Cuba as in Ireland, where all work stops for a funeral and where sometimes they dig up noble corpses in order to bury them again. *Patria o muerte!* Fatherland or death! Said Martí: 'To die is nothing; to die is to live; to die is to plant.' And the first stanza of the national anthem, *La Bayamese* (1868), declares: 'To die for the Fatherland is to live.' The great enemy then was Spain, today it is America, and tomorrow ... Such an anthem has need of mortal foes, who become the very parameters of a meaningful national identity. The poet José Alvarez Baragaño, who died suddenly in 1962 at the age of thirty, wrote: 'My one eternal engagement is with death.' But such expressions make poor poetry and even poorer philosophy—the eloquence of death is that it speaks for itself.

In a small town we stop for lunch at a hotel run by INIT but packed with honeymoon couples looking faintly furtive and ashamed about their graduation. For once the bar is at ground level and has windows looking on to the street, thus attracting a great throng of small boys who tap on the glass, grimace, offer gestures whose meaning can only be guessed at, and generally make one uneasy about swallowing a sickly-sweet crème-de-menthe mixed with rum in ice. Almost all Cuban cocktails are pretty, brightly coloured, feminine, and without after-effects. For Martha it is all too good to be true and she measures Cuba by the miles between the bars. But

'Eming-way' carries a black tongue thirsting for a man-sized scotch which he cannot afford (not being 'Eming-way').

We head now for the capital of Oriente and Cuba's second city, Santiago de Cuba, but stop off on the way at Bayamo to inspect a new housing complex of twenty-five hundred people, half of whom are children. Admittedly this is a show-place, the familiar trap of the conducted tour but, on the other hand, it isn't a mirage or a magic lantern, and it certainly wasn't erected merely to impress passing clusters of tourists. Seduction-centre though Bayamo is, the people it successfully entices are the peasants of Oriente, who, if they will only abandon their private farms and their private attitudes, if they will only throw in their lot with a co-operative, are welcomed here by a complex of landscaped apartment blocks, free furniture, radio and television sets, excellent schools (teacher–pupil ratio, one to thirty), a well-equipped clinic, shops, services, and wages running from a hundred and thirty-five to a hundred and eighty pesos a month.

We are shown an apartment. The occupant greets us politely but without enthusiasm. 'They always show my apartment,' she says.

'Why,' someone asks her, 'is it the best?'

Carlos translates.

'Oh no,' she says. 'But I don't make a fuss so they go on showing my apartment.' She shrugs. 'At least I have to keep it clean.'

Corralled in a small living-room, twenty of us stand and shift about awkwardly like cattle herded into a small pen. Martha and I both feel embarrassed and I am reminded of the days when as a soldier I was obliged every morning to fold my blankets into the shape of a cut-through Swiss roll while an officer peered closely to see if any of the jam was dripping. What are we doing? Hunting for specks of dust? Fingering the plastic table-cloth for bread crumbs?

Searching for icons under the bed? Measuring the bed?

Outside we are welcomed by a representative of the Communist Party. Monsieur Lepinay wants to know how many Party members there are at Bayamo.

'Eighty-five.'

'Out of two thousand five hundred people?'

'Yes. One adult in fifteen, to be precise.'

'That is not a Party of the masses,' comments Monsieur Lepinay (in whose country the poor Communists have to count votes).

'It will be. We are in no hurry. The quality of the vanguard is important.'

The Young Swiss wants to know whether Party members enjoy any special privileges. Nicole scowls and tells the Young Swiss that he doesn't understand anything. The Young Swiss looks sullen and the Cubans do not feel the need to add to his pain. I therefore remark, as politely as possible, that the question is an interesting one and that if we had thought it could be answered on the Left Bank of Paris we would have travelled not to Cuba but to the Left Bank of Paris. Carlos, though never inclined to force the pace of a confrontation, really welcomes any sign of life, and so takes about ten minutes to translate the gist of what I have said to a growing group of interested Cubans. Something gets lost down the line, for our Communist representative then answers, very decisively, that Cuban Communists enjoy no more privileges than Parisian Communists.

'Except,' he adds, to laughter, 'they must work harder than anyone else. In the fields during the day, and in committees at night.' He winks. 'We hardly ever sleep. Look at me, wasting away. Perhaps you will take me for a holiday to Paris.'

We are all routed and drift, snapping pictures, back to the coach.

*   *   *

Perched on high ground overlooking Santiago, El Ranch Hotel is of a peculiarly pleasant design quite common among Cuban hotels built in expansive garden settings. One complex houses the restaurant, boutique, bar, and management; the guests' bedrooms consist of terraced, ground-floor cabins spreading out like the spokes of a wheel through the gardens, with sloping tiled roofs and colourful shutters over the windows. It all puts me in mind of Mr Michener's Hawaii, and I keep an eye open for anything moving through the palm trees in a grass skirt.

Alas, it is merely the Old Swiss trundling to his cabin in a shirt which has now seen ten days' wear and—God preserve us from the thought—maybe ten nights' as well. Certainly the women are beginning to confer about this scandal but they mistake gossip for action. Imagine my astonishment, then, when my wife enters our cabin holding between the tips of her fingers a radioactive garment which—I am backing into a corner—is, must be, The Shirt!

'Great Scott! Did he put up a fight?'

Deigning not to answer, our Nana vanishes into the bathroom carrying a flask of soap powder, a selection of my underclothes—and The Shirt.

'But you can't wash them together!' I wail.

Comes only the running of (lukewarm) water for an answer.

We take our places for dinner while a handsome baritone sings of love and death. In a state of unbearable tension I await the arrival of a naked Old Swiss. Storm clouds hover low in the sky, mosquitoes whine, and it is quite clear that The Shirt will not dry by morning. Normally the Old Swiss is the first à table, tucking his napkin into The Shirt and wolfing bread-rolls with such gusto that Carlos, Rafael, and Pedro (Rafael is always the ringleader in this delinquency) collapse in helpless laughter. Now we are all seated, except the Old Swiss. One place empty. I glower at my heartless wife, whose serenity remains unruffled. Then! Roll of thunder, roll of drums! He comes! In a brand new, clean check shirt! There is a spontaneous outburst of applause. Rafael disappears under the table. Mystified, the Old Swiss looks scornfully about him, shrugs and begins to wolf bread-rolls. Carlos and Pedro join Rafael under the table.

Over coffee a waiter offers us fat cigars at ten cents each. At the bar the same cigars cost one peso. That's socialism.

After dinner we gather in the garden, with the lights of the harbour glinting below and the thunderclouds drifting beyond the mountains. Evidently, by tacit agreement, we are about to have our first serious group discussion. Nicole begins by saying that she is sure we have many questions to ask Carlos, and then delivers a long and exquisite apologia on behalf of the Cuban Revolution. The Young Swiss, still a few miles short of the oasis where Virginian cigarettes grow on trees and the lemonade springs, lifts a bunch of mine and mutters 'crap, man' in my ear.

After a short, deferential silence, Monsieur Lepinay takes the Cuban bull by the horns and offers us the perspective of a 'higher technician' and a 'dedicated militant'. His exposition is studded with such phrases as 'frontiers of under-development', 'infantile leftism', 'imperialist contradictions', and 'solidarity of peoples'. The words *Union soviétique* frequently cross his tongue and I gather that they are good words; the word *Chine* is used more sparingly and with studied ambiguity. The theories of guerrilla warfare propounded by Guevara and Régis Debray are acclaimed for their nobility but marked down for impracticality.

Nicole replies. With a logic, a clarity of phrase, and a precision to which only the French can aspire, she indicates that the French Communist Party is a bunch of creeps. Hence their betrayal of the May 1968 Revolution in Paris. Hence this, hence that. Thoroughly henced, Monsieur Lepinay sucks his pipe calmly, gazes down at the harbour, and prepares to demolish this infantile leftist, this pseudo-revolutionary, modish *fille à papa*. Meanwhile the rest of us, humble spectators to this brilliant duel (or, as one may suspect, duet), have plenty of time to isolate and ponder certain questions. Let us take one of them: Cuba's relations with Russia and China.

There are plenty of Russians in Cuba—enough for little boys in the street to ask, as a first guess, '*Russo?*' You find Soviet technicians and their families wherever there are swimming-pools, soaking up all the sun before Monsieur Lepinay can grab some. Other Russians come on eleven-day package tours before moving on to France and Morocco. How did all this begin?

It began with Cuba's estrangement from the United States. In February 1960 Mikoyan visited Havana to open a Soviet scientific exhibition, and a trade agreement was signed. The Russians promised a two hundred and eighty million dollar loan over a twelve-year period; the same year, seventeen hundred Cuban students set out for the Soviet bloc. But the Russians were cautious. They knew, understood, and in a sense controlled the (Communist) Popular Socialist Party, but the bearded *barbudos* with their rifles and extravagant ambitions were a puzzle. Not until April 1962 did the Soviet Press first refer to Castro as 'comrade'. When Castro turned on the Communist leader Escalante, the Russians had to swallow their loyalties and support Castro.

Then Khrushchev lost his head. He sent missiles to Cuba. Kennedy forced him to back down and the American pledge not to invade Cuba remained informal because Castro refused to allow the United Nations to inspect the missile sites. The Cubans were completely disgusted by Russia's abject retreat; in the middle of the crisis Castro remarked at the University of Havana that Khrushchev lacked balls (*cojones*). Relations cooled. But economic necessity prevailed. In April 1963 Castro visited Moscow. By 1965, forty-seven per cent of

Cuban exports were heading for the USSR, and forty per cent of imports came from the same source. Cuba had already accumulated a trade deficit with Russia of about one hundred and fifty million dollars, and with Czechoslovakia (which supplies Cuba with arms) one of over fifty million. Meanwhile, friendly relations were established with China; the Cubans showed themselves reluctant to be drawn into the widening Sino-Soviet split. Facing a Cuban trade deficit with China of over thirty million dollars, Guevara visited Peking in 1965. By the following year something seemed to have gone wrong; Castro criticized the Chinese for failing to meet rice deliveries and, for good measure, castigated Mao for his 'senile barbarism' and for having instituted in China a form of fascism.

At this stage the Cubans were in a pretty desperate state, since at a political level Castro was also quarrelling with Russia. Soviet caution over Vietnam was one cause of friction; Soviet disapproval of Cuba's Permanent Revolution doctrine (Guevara in Bolivia, etc.) was another. Cuba emphasized her independence in 1968 by refusing to sign the nuclear non-proliferation treaty which, said Foreign Minister Raúl Roa, would further divide the world into the possessing and non-possessing nations. At this stage, and with the Tri-Continental Congress in Havana, Cuba was clearly bidding for leadership among the non-aligned nations of the Third World rather than signing up for membership of the Soviet-led 'Socialist bloc'.

The big change came in 1968. Guevara's death imposed a reappraisal of revolutionary perspectives in Latin America. Castro, like Stalin before him, began to think in terms of 'socialism in one country'. When the French students almost brought down de Gaulle in May 1968 (many of them carrying Guevara banners), Havana remained studiously silent. (France was supplying Cuba with valuable agricultural machinery on generous credit terms.) The Communist-led

Cuban Student Federation did not even send a symbolic message of solidarity to their colleagues battling *les flics* round the Sorbonne. Perhaps, more ominous, and more of a domestic betrayal, was Castro's staunch silence about the bloody repression of the Mexican protest demonstrations during the summer of 1968. (Sartre and Russell, it may be recalled, pleaded for an Olympic boycott of Mexico.) And yet the Mexican students who demonstrated on 26 July did so expressly to honour the example of Cuba. Who, now, lacked *cojones*?

Then came Czechoslovakia. During the spring of liberalization associated with the leadership of Alexander Dubček, the Cuban Press had printed both sides of the argument between Prague and Moscow (vigorously supported by Ulbricht in East Berlin). When on 22 August the forces of the Warsaw Pact invaded Czechoslovakia and seized its leaders, the whole Cuban nation expected Castro to denounce this act of naked imperialism. After all, the simplest mind could see the obvious implications: what is sauce for the Czechoslovak goose is sauce for the Cuban gander—or so those big eaters, Russia and America, might easily agree. On the day of the invasion Czechoslovak technicians marched through the Varadero district of Havana, shouting '*patria o muerte*', and were warmly cheered.

When Castro finally spoke on television the whole nation was dumbfounded. (Indeed it is my impression that even today sensitive Cubans remain shell-shocked about it.) Castro admitted that Czechoslovak sovereignty had been violated without a shred of legal justification—the Soviet pretext, that Prague had called in the Warsaw Pact to defend socialism, he dismissed as worthless. But, he continued, the Russians had acted promptly to avert a greater evil, the resurgence of capitalism in Czechoslovakia, and he warned against any weakening of the revolutionary spirit in Eastern Europe. Four years later *Granma* was printing computer-dictated articles supporting the new wave of trials in Prague, attacking as 'reactionary' those who protested against them, and concealing the fact that the Western Communist Parties were deeply disturbed by the image of Communism they fostered.

Soviet aid is worth a million dollars a day (which, by the way, is not the same as a million dollars a day; Cuba desperately needs hard convertible currency). Since 1968 Cuba has given Russia no trouble. When one remembers how back in 1960 both Jean-Paul Sartre and C. Wright Mills insisted that these brash, anarchic, idealistic young rebels would never join forces with the cunning, compromising, power-hungry Stalinists, one can only wince. I do not believe that we can lay the blame for this distressing mutation at the door of the United States; as Sartre said, if the United States had not existed, the Cuban Revolution would have had to invent her. The villain of the piece is history; its sluggish pace; its stark dichotomy of scarcity and need; its exhausted soil; its grim refusal to keep pace with philosophy; its human human beings.

Well, if I claim that I am thinking all this out while paying close attention to the debate between Nicole and Monsieur Lepinay, then you are right, I'm not. The sky is clear now and the cicadas are noisy; the Old Swiss is happy in his clean shirt, Madame Bourgeois has fallen asleep clutching a pile of treasures from the boutique, and no one has yet asked a question about Cuba. The French ask answers, not questions, and Carlos is growing restless. Rafael has wandered away to get rid of the last beer and to drink another one. During a short pause in the endless dialogue between Nicole and Monsieur L., Carlos intervenes with a demand that I forthwith express the English point of view.

I ask him to explain the Cuban position on Czechoslovakia. He repeats, word for word, the latest editorial in *Granma*. I ask him whether, on any occasion, he has seen fit to hold an opinion different from *Granma*'s. Nicole says I am implying that Cubans are incapable of thinking for themselves—an old imperialist *canard*. Madame Lepinay, brightening up now, interjects with great relevance:

'And what about the oppression of the Irish people?'

'But surely you would rather discuss Cuba.'

'Ireland,' says Carlos, with a chuckle.

Madame Lepinay is already extremely angry about my (as yet unexpressed) opinions on Ireland. How can I complain of Soviet action in Czechoslovakia when, at this very minute, just as the Americans are bombing Haiphong, British troops in Belfast and Londonderry are decimating the Irish people? How?

I mention one aspect of the crisis: that whereas a majority of the people of Ulster are determined to remain part of the United Kingdom, a majority of the Czechoslovak people, in so far as my understanding permits, do not wish to remain part of the USSR.

Carlos says that the whole Irish people should be granted self-determination.

'But that would mean civil war.'

'Very well. We had a civil war here, you know.'

'It was also a class war. In Ireland it would be a religious war.'

Nicole dismisses this as a mystification of the real issue: the concerted attempt by British and Irish capitalists to divide, and therefore rule, the entire Irish working class, whether Catholic or Protestant.

Carlos judges this analysis to be correct. Madame Lepinay adds: 'And what about Princess Margaret? She is a million-airess, yes?'

'I expect so.'

'And the Queen, how wealthy is she?'

'I'm afraid I don't know.'

'Richer than Batista, eh?'

'I expect so.'

'David,' says Carlos, 'for whom do you vote?'

'Carlos, for whom do *you* vote?'

Groupings of stars familiar from childhood astronomy lessons glitter overhead, but of the country on which they now shine we learn very little. The sterility of polemic, the fog of evasion, the acidity of a French Marxism which barely conceals a rampant chauvinism—we are all proving that we are too old and wise to be wrong. After a further hour or so of this we drift back to our cabins wrapped in self-righteousness. Some time after sleep finally claims us we are wakened by weird howls in the night, followed by a determined thumping on our door. I leap up, convinced that it is the Old Swiss come to demand The Shirt. The ghastly, fatigued features of Madame Bourgeois confront me in the moonlight.

'Monsieur, have you had breakfast?'

'No, madame, it's one o'clock in the morning.'

'Then it's time for lunch?'

'In the *morning*, madame.'

'The night, eh? You mean the night?'

'Yes.'

'Everyone has disappeared, monsieur.'

'Only to bed. What is your room number, madame?'

'I have forgotten ... so many hotels, monsieur, so many room numbers.'

'Please show me your key ring.'

Eventually, clawing aside thick wads of money, she locates it. I guide her to her room. She is about to tip me but thinks better of it. As she turns I see that her eyes are moist.

'Monsieur, what town is this?'

'Santiago, madame.'

She nods and closes the door.

Santiago is attractive. Lined with trees and rich in open spaces—not areas of arbitrary desolation but planned spaces

—it is a comfortable and comforting city. At the cemetery we pay homage to José Martí, whose ornate rotunda, built in 1915 and bearing the shields of the six provinces, dominates its more humble neighbours. Once more on the move, we pass through a gigantic housing estate built to accommodate thirteen thousand people, its apartment blocks set at angles, erected out of pre-cast blocks and decorated with attractive fretwork patterns resembling lace. Tropical architecture gains some of its ease and openness from the blessings of the climate, particularly the absence of snow, frost, and the ensuing thaw. The Revolution has inspired young Cuban architects to admirable feats of ingenuity, but they, like the Director of the Museum at Camagüey, suffer from the country's isolation, from a lack of contact with foreign colleagues, from shortage of travel funds, and even from the difficulty of obtaining foreign architectural journals. Nevertheless, a major attribute of the régime has been its refusal to equate virtue and social utility with ugliness, or, alternatively, to translate monumental progress into ponderous, monumental architecture. The Cubans have captured or echoed something of the adventurous aesthetic spirit which promised so much in Bolshevik Russia before it was snuffed out.

Nor, architecturally speaking, must one forget the past. In Santiago we are taken to a splendid old colonial house in a state of meticulous preservation, graced with richly carved wooden ceilings (still a notable feature of Cuban building) and furnished with good, solid, bourgeois tables, chairs, and desks derived from Spanish, French, and English styles. Also on view are some pretty creole plates and jugs, dating from the seventeenth century.

In the towns one hardly ever sees a policeman (though the fact that police and militia wear similar green uniforms increases the possibility of mis-identification). The traffic seems to be self-disciplined (which certainly can't be said for little Israel), and the pedestrians cross the streets when and where they please.

In a little atelier devoted to woodwork we come upon some ladies rubbing little pieces of coloured wood against electric lathes and then glueing them in charming designs to cigar boxes, wooden trays, and what have you. In the rear of the workshop wicker-work baskets and chairs are taking shape. An old craftsman, seeing that I smoke a pipe, fashions a new one before my very eyes—then admits that mine is better. Here the minimum wage is ninety pesos a month, lower than in the rural co-operative at Bayamo and thus an accurate reflection of prevailing priorities. Before the Revolution the unionized proletarian was the aristocrat of Cuba's wage-earners; today it is the peasant. Seeing many stools empty, I assume that we have again encountered the shift system, but Carlos explains that most of the workers are visiting the hospital for a routine vaccination.

If our visit to Santiago begins at a modest pace, the next day brings a different tempo. At last our moment has arrived to move in the shadow of heroes, to trace step by bloody step the emergence of the new Cuba, to storm the Moncada Barracks as Fidel once did, and to breathe with him the thin, dry air of the Sierra Maestra. History, legend, myth, and the imagination coalesce to recreate one of the most remarkable odysseys of our time.

Castro: let us recall a few facts about his early years. He was born on his father's plantation near Birán on the north coast of Oriente. His father, Angel Castro y Argiz, was a self-made man; once an immigrant labourer from Galicia, in Spain, he had accumulated estates of 23,300 acres, married twice and sired nine children. Fidel, born on 13 August 1927 to his father's second wife, was the fifth of the nine. He was illegitimate at birth but his parents married soon afterwards.

From the outset he was a hothead, impetuous, self-assured, and dominating. In 1947 he joined an expedition of Cubans and Dominicans who planned to overthrow Generalissimo Rafael Trujillo, dictator of the Dominican Republic, but the project was squelched at the start by President Grau San Martín of Cuba. The following year Fidel married Mirta Díaz-Balart; their son Fidelito (who remains in Cuba) was born in 1949. This marriage—Fidel's first and last—broke up a few years later during his imprisonment after the Moncada fiasco.

The Moncada Barracks, a low, unimposing complex of buildings now painted pink, was at that time (1953) the head-quarters of Batista's garrison in Santiago. From all over Cuba Fidel brought together one hundred and sixty-seven rebels, two of them women, and then announced to them his master plan: to seize simultaneously the Barracks, the Civil Hospital, and the Palace of Justice in Santiago, whereupon the people would be invited to rise. But the plan was not a sound one. The attackers could ill afford to split their meagre forces in this way, and on the day everything went wrong. One group got lost, another was surprised, a third took the hospital and then waited to be captured. Fidel and his brother Raúl escaped, but the carnage was terrible.

Part of the Barracks is now a museum. Walking over these scrubbed flagstones one can visualize the pools of blood, the cruel thud of bullets ripping into flesh and bone, the lurching bodies, the screams of the wounded. A gallery of horrific photographs confirms the worst fears of the imagination— sprawled on the floor, propped against the wall, the dead and the dying, bloody and mutilated. The eye strives to escape to other, more reassuring pictures of a serene Guevara showing the light to peasant guerrillas in the Sierra Maestra four years later, but the stench of carnage remains inescapable. To die for the Fatherland is to live. To *live*? Is Fidel not haunted by the thought that he, leader and survivor, was the one who really lived? Perhaps so, for even today he period-ically returns to the subject of Moncada, castigating his own ineptitude and urging all Cubans not to forget those who fell. His second-in-command, Santa María, for example: before they killed him Batista's men plucked out one of his eyes and carried it to his captive sister, Haydée, inviting her to talk. She refused and her brother died. Today she is Director of La Casa de las Américas.

A few days after Castro's escape from the holocaust of Moncada, he was captured in the foothills of the Sierra while sleeping off his exhaustion. The officer who took him spared his life because he knew his father. In the interval, the policy of savage reprisal had been reversed and Castro got away with a trial rather than a summary execution. He spent twenty-two months on the Isle of Pines (where he now sends his own political prisoners) and used the time to read voraciously and eclectically: St Thomas Aquinas, John of Salisbury, Luther, Knox, Milton, Rousseau, and Tom Paine —any notable authority he could lay hands on. It is said that Marx and Lenin did not figure prominently in his readings.

Released from prison under a general amnesty, he returned to Havana and resumed his role as agitator. Batista promptly banned him from the radio and from addressing public meetings, the consequence being that Castro withdrew to Mexico to foment a new armed insurrection. Harassed by the Mexican police and Foreign Ministry, he and his comrades were saved from expulsion (it is believed) only by the intervention of ex-President Lázaro Cárdenas of Mexico. It was in Mexico that he first met up with an Argentinian doctor called Ernesto Guevara, who had fled from Guatemala after a CIA-engineered coup overthrew the leftist régime of Arbenz. Although the two men prepared for a protracted campaign of guerrilla warfare in Cuba, strangely enough they remained ignorant of Mao Tse-tung's classic treatise on the subject until after the summer offensive against Batista in 1958.

Carlos glances at his watch and we are summoned back to the coach. Walking away from Moncada along the stone paving between neat beds of flowers one glances obliquely at the soldiers moving about in leisurely work parties, one scans their faces and sees not only the mutilated faces of the rebel soldiers who died on these same flagstones but also the blank, impassive faces of the Batista soldiers who posed for photographs round the corpses. Man changes inwardly less rapidly and less radically than he sometimes supposes. Twelve kilometres outside Santiago we come to the little chicken farm (a bungalow really) near Siboney where the conspirators had gathered before the disastrous assault. Here, too, a spirit of reverential preservation prevails: green uniforms, the well in the garden where arms were hidden, a photograph of Fidel being interrogated after his capture by Santiago's chief of police, and a subsequent picture taken as he walked out of prison in a double-breasted suit, beardless and slightly double-chinned.

The road winds up a steep gradient into the foothills of the Sierra Maestra, and one quickly realizes the advantage accruing to a force, however small, entrenched in the dense woodlands on the upper slopes. Arriving at a restaurant near the summit we put to work a cook we have specially transported for the purpose, and then spend a couple of hours waiting for lunch, admiring the view, feeling our way into guerrilla boots, imagining the grinding engines of a pursuing army, and trying unsuccessfully to catch sight of the Jamaican coastline. Not so far away, Carlos points out, lies the American base at Guantánamo Bay; but the curve of enmity is concealed by the rolling blue hills and by that vast disdainful silence which pulls men upwards and away from their own misanthropy.

Back to Castro. In October 1955 he was in the United States, lecturing and raising money, at a time when the rest of us were watching James Dean and Marilyn Monroe. Then, finally, on 25 November 1956, eighty-two men packed into a little motor launch called *Granma*, which could comfortably accommodate twelve men, and which now lies proudly at rest in Havana harbour. They encountered rough seas. Seasick, hungry and thirsty, they hove to on 2 December between Niquero and Cabo Cruz, late, in the wrong place, out of touch with Cuban support forces led by Frank País, and, worst of all, to be greeted by an alerted army. Landing in marshland, Fidel experienced yet another catastrophe, with the greater part of his force killed or captured. The survivors wandered for days like hunted animals. Eventually Guevara, though gravely wounded in the neck, met up with Castro.

The theory of guerrilla warfare is that it serves as a catalyst to a discontented peasantry who, emboldened by the first successful skirmishes, join the rebel forces and so contribute to greater victories. Guillermo García was the first genuine peasant to join Fidel's tiny force and, gratitude being what it is, not to mention revolutionary theory, is now commander of the armed forces of the three western provinces, as well as a member of the eleven-man Communist Party politburo.

The first minor victory came on 17 January 1957 at La Plata. Batista then despatched a force of twelve thousand troops, together with modern armament and spotter planes. But the Sierra Maestra is a wooded region of three thousand square miles, and it is the apparently helpless guerrilla who, supremely vigilant, never sleeping twice in the same place, never trusting the friendship of a strange peasant, keeping constantly on the move, is able to choose his moment, his place of ambush, and so simultaneously capture arms and demoralize his pursuers. So it was. Meanwhile, Frank País, the leader of the Fidelista forces in Santiago and by all accounts a man of rare nobility and courage, was captured and killed in July 1957. One woman, Celia Sánchez, who had collaborated with País and whose presence among them was accepted by the mountain-goat guerrillas reluctantly, fought at their side for almost two years. She has since become Fidel's alter ego, confidante, housekeeper, and cabinet minister. Such people, lucid, brave, and persistent, comrades who remain faithful to each other and to their task, however rough the seas, constitute a natural élite, the cream of any nation's milk. Only particular quirks of fate and configurations of history can dictate whether they shall be mourned as martyrs, like País and Santa María, or revered as the guardians of a new political culture. But their self-assumed trusteeship carries, naturally, the danger of oligarchy.

Fidel's father died in 1956 before the *Granma* landing, but had he lived there is little doubt that he would have disowned his son's undertaking. Castro's mother and his elder brother Ramón deeply disapproved, though Ramón did reluctantly help Fidel during the campaign, assuming that its objective was merely to overthrow a tyranny. In May 1959 the Castro family plantations were included in the break-up of the big *latifundia*; mother and brother were outraged. Later Ramón was again reconciled with Fidel and took charge of agrarian reform in Oriente. But the youngest sibling, Juana, remained implacably hostile, and in 1962-63 Fidel had to close his eyes to the fact that she and her mother were in touch with counter-revolutionaries. Finally, he allowed Juana to go into exile with all her possessions; once in America, she bitterly denounced him.

Fidel Castro is simultaneously Prime Minister, First Secretary of the Communist Party, Minister-President of the Institute for Agrarian Reform, and Commander-in-Chief of the Armed Forces. (Osvaldo Dorticós has been President of the Republic since 1959.) This is an alarming concentration of power and prestige in one man's hands, and it is probably true to say that with the exception of Mao no Communist leader since Stalin has held so many strings of state or has enjoyed such unrivalled pre-eminence. Fidel, *líder* and *jefe máximo*, is at the time of writing only forty-seven years old, in the prime of life, as self-confident, self-willed, and self-propelled as ever, a natural leader incapable of taking orders and only rarely capable of accepting advice. Though he, more than any other man, 'made' the Revolution, he emerges, paradoxically, as the main obstacle to its completion, to a genuinely democratic devolution of power to the people through representative institutions.

In the meantime, the Cuban people remain *his* children. At the end of the printed version of the Second Declaration of Havana one reads: 'The multitude raise their hands with a prolonged ovation and they sing the Cuban National Anthem and the International.' Each great speech is greeted with 'unanimous approval'. A few years ago Castro himself drew a self-serving distinction between the crazed, emotional hypnotized mobs of the fascist dictatorships and the critical, rational, analytical spirit of Cuban audiences. And one must admit that his long speeches amount to far more than hymns of hate or calls to destiny. They are packed with facts, evidence, practical details, confessions of failure, rational designs. In all sincerity he wants to educate his people, to share his thoughts with them, to generate a dialogue. But 'dialogue' is a fancy word. Castro is like a loving, intelligent, and autocratic father who, when he has decided what is best for his children, comes to them, sits them on his lap and asks them gently to express their own wishes. 'Don't be afraid, speak up!' For a while he listens to their half-baked, muddled notions with a great show of respect and attentiveness, puffing at his cigar, nodding here, clarifying a point there. And then, when they have finished, he 'persuades' them precisely why they really want to do what he wants them to do.

Up here in the pine-wooded hills the sun is hot. I wriggle

into the shade and doze. Presently Carlos sits down beside me, bringing a friend, a big fellow, still young, with close-cropped hair and a face like a shock-absorber. Carlos introduces Manuel.

'You wanted to meet a real guerrilla, David?'

'Of course.'

'Manuel is my friend. He fought with Camillo Cienfuegos here in the Sierra, and later in the capture of Santa Clara.'

Manuel nods modestly, picking out the words 'Cienfuegos', 'Sierra', and 'Santa Clara' from Carlos's French. I regard Manuel with awe, searching his features, his hands, for scars. One of the originals! In the great tradition of Garibaldi, Bolívar, and Zapata, a Gunman of the People!

'Please ask him what he thinks of the Revolution now. I mean, has it turned out as he expected, as he hoped it would?'

Carlos asks. Manuel answers in a few forceful phrases.

'Things are very good now. There were some difficult times. Some comrades became disappointed, they felt betrayed by Fidel, they went to America.'

'When he fought with Cienfuegos here in these hills, did Manuel realize it would be a socialist revolution?'

Carlos asks. Manuel scratches his head; at this altitude such questions are onerous.

'There was much discussion of these things within the 26 July Movement. Many opinions. Some very sincere men thought it would be a bourgeois revolution. Each man had his own idea of what the Revolution would be.'

'Yes. Yes, of course. In the Sierra days Fidel did not speak publicly as a socialist. I wondered whether he spoke privately as a socialist ... among the comrades.'

Carlos is uncertain whether to translate directly or to rephrase the question with comments of his own. Both men are trying to remember whether my facts are correct; am I laying some kind of trap? Manuel speaks defensively, with a hint of irritation, his eyes focused across the blue hills.

'Fidel himself has said that he had to overcome certain petty-bourgeois prejudices of his own. The Revolution was a school for us all.'

The time has come to drop this line of questioning. The historian and the journalist constantly encounter such disappointments. Having studied the available documents, the printed sources, they set out eagerly in pursuit of eyewitnesses. Who merely scratch their heads. Imagine:

'King Richard III, thank you for granting me this interview. I have tracked you down across five centuries and I notice your humpback is not so prominent as the books suggest. Could you please clear up one small problem: was it you who murdered the little princes in the Tower?'

'People believe what they want to believe.'

'Quite so, sire. But what should they believe?'

'Whatever pleases their imaginations.'

'Could you please cast your mind back to that year—1483.'

Pause.

'Hm ... there was a good deal of unrest in the country ... things were not easy at all.'

'Yes, sire, so we historians have gathered. But the little princes, your nephews ... in the Tower. How did they die?'

'I believe there were conflicting reports.'

I ask Manuel, now, whether he ever met Che Guevara. Manuel brightens up. Yes, he did. Che was a very remarkable man. No one like him. His death a terrible loss.

'His asthma was, of course, a tremendous handicap?'

'Of course. Sometimes his suffering was great. But luckily he was a doctor himself and knew what to do.'

'And Cienfuegos, how did he die?'

'In a plane crash.'

'The cause?'

Manuel shrugs. 'It is not clear.'

Now Manuel rises (he is very tall) and throws a laughing remark to Carlos. Apparently he is offering to present me with a genuine guerrilla forage cap. I shake his hand, delighted. He departs. A day passes. *Mañana* is a Cuban notion as much as a Spanish notion, and tomorrow's tomorrow is as good as tomorrow. But, sure enough, two days later, Manuel appears at El Ranch Hotel, plonks a cap on my head, smiles, offers me his huge hand, and is gone. Examining the cap, I am a little disappointed, believing that I had been promised a sweat-stained veteran's cap actually worn during the Sierra campaign. But this one is brand new, indistinguishable from those worn by thousands of militia-men, and three sizes too small for my head. Later, returning to London and finding that it exactly fits my nine-year-old son, I will present it to him with an elaborate and awesome explanation, persuade him to locate Cuba on the globe, and finally try to explain the difference between a guerrilla and a gorilla. He wears it regularly to school, but will soon have to hand it on to his younger brother, also a very keen gorilla.

We descend to Santiago harbour and its surrounding bays. Here the decisive naval battle between Spain and America was fought in 1902, and here also, Carlos points out, counter-revolutionary terrorists landed as recently as 1970 with a view to sabotage. But the psychic strains of a violent history cannot be sustained indefinitely. We call it a day and head for a beachcamp where Monsieur Lepinay finds an empty swimming-pool, gesticulates his dismay eloquently, then plunges into the salt sea. A *'Caballeros'* for the men, a *'Damas'* for the ladies, a snoozing lifeguard perched in an umpire's chair for the unlucky. The Old Swiss rolls up his trousers and wades in; even Madame Bourgeois gets her ankles wet, but she refuses to part with her purse, even in the sea. Nicole proves to be a fish, Carlos a dolphin. The Young Swiss, cigarette in mouth, emits a final yodel then vanishes beneath the waves. Martha's hair is tied up with a red ribbon and I sit with my back to a palm tree (rather a thin one) trying to trace the passage of this red ribbon and vaguely composing letters of consolation to its owner's mother.

CHAPTER
5

Santa Clara, Varadero,
The Bay of Pigs, Pinar del Río

Our destination is Santa Clara, capital of Las Villas. Rafael and Pedro drive very well; they inspire confidence. But any attempt to sleep in the coach is invariably interrupted by the violent wail of its horn. The occasion of this is rarely an obstinate tractor, a stray cow, or an oncoming vehicle; almost inevitably it means that Rafael has caught sight of a girl of marriageable age. The *machismo* of the machine is an authentic indicator of underdevelopment, the ready rule of thumb being that in developed countries drivers tend to slow down when they enter villages or towns, whereas in underdeveloped countries they speed up, sound their horn aggressively, and generally dare any living thing to cross their path. In *Bech: A Book*, John Updike has a cruelly observant story about a Rumanian chauffeur whom the wheel of a car transformed from a gentle family man into a fascist slaughterer.

Martha and I take it in turns to sit beside the window. The privilege, however, is becoming somewhat academic since we can no longer see out of the windows, so caked are they with the mud of the daily storms. Stubborn in my insistence that the purpose of a sight-seeing tour is to see the sights,

I hesitantly begin to sound out opinion. Everyone concurs but the prevailing mood is one of resigned acceptance. Monsieur Lepinay agrees with me that it is 'incredible' and adds that a Communist coach-driver in France would be expelled from the Party for such dereliction of duty. Would Monsieur Lepinay therefore consider speaking to Nicole about it? Monsieur Lepinay might; but I detect in Monsieur Lepinay a reluctance to extend his quarrel with the New Left from the subject of foreign policy to that of coach windows.

'We can't even wave to the volunteer brigades,' I say sulkily.

At our first stop I climb out of the coach and ostentatiously survey the windows.

'A lot of mud,' I say to Carlos.

He nods. 'It's the storms.'

'Difficult to see out.'

He nods again with something of that placid stubbornness which characterizes the Russian 'nyet'—meaning, things are what they are. 'They will be cleaned soon,' he promises.

But they aren't. I begin to brood. In my opinion, Rafael and Pedro are scarcely worked to the limit. One of them travels as a sleeping passenger and large parts of the day are spent doing absolutely nothing. I embark on a new grievance tour. Word reaches Nicole.

'I hear you have been complaining about the windows,' she says.

'One can't see a thing. It's like a dungeon in here.'

'Please understand that this is a very wet time of year.'

'Couldn't some of the water be used to clean the windows?'

'When we reach a special garage with the proper equipment.'

In despair, I sit down next to the Young Swiss. At last I am his disciple, his slave: without private enterprise and competition there is no hope. We compare notes on all the big, gleaming windows we have seen on American and European coaches. Would any private company dare to display its name under mud-caked windows? No, it would not, and the Young Swiss takes the occasion to borrow a few cigarettes. It is very hot and I am losing my reason. Mealtimes now madden me. For hour after hour Pedro and Rafael sit in the shade, sipping beer and lighting cigarettes, totally unabashed to be the custodians of a wheeled hippopotamus looking as if it had just waded out of the Zambesi shallows.

Choking with rage I once again mention the matter to Carlos. 'There are facilities at Santa Clara,' he says.

'Facilities? Listen, let me have a pail of water and a rag and I'll wash the windows myself.'

The French contingent (smug, cowardly bastards) are watching intently. At last the Englishman has gone over the edge—it was always on the cards.

Nicole says that if I were to wash the windows myself it would be an insult to Rafael and Pedro.

'Perhaps they would be less insulted if they joined me in the work.'

'It is not their job to wash the windows.'

'For God's sake—isn't this the country of the volunteer brigade, of personal initiative? Isn't this the country where everyone lends a hand when something needs to be done?'

I turn and stump away. This is terrible! I have lost all sense of proportion, I am saying things that will never be forgiven! A group of strangers travelling in claustrophobic contact with one another for three weeks must, above all, keep a tight rein on their tempers. Martha looks distraught but recognizes that in this mood I am beyond her comfort or counsel. And since I now childishly decline even to eat lunch, no doubt the overture to a hunger strike, she has to sit at table beside an empty place and bear on her own shoulders the shame and humiliation of marriage to a lunatic.

The next morning the windows are clean.

'You see,' Rafael says as I climb into the coach, 'all for you.' But he doesn't call me 'Eming-way'.

Now I feel guilty.

We stop off at a pineapple plantation. Sitting under a shade-roof of thatch supported by bamboo poles, we consume thin slices of pineapple sprinkled with salt while the director of the plantation furnishes us with statistics and explains that each plant produces fruit four or five times in its life. Very interesting—in time a group of travellers becomes almost immune to information. Munch, munch.

Madame Bourgeois was last seen fast asleep in the coach. Attempts to rouse her with promises of the delicious 'ananas' had failed. But now, once again waking up to find herself alone and deserted at no certain time of day or night, maybe in this country, maybe in that, she stumbles towards us cross-eyed, and then, seeing the sliced pineapples, asks whether we bought them 'in the boutique'. The Cubans collapse. Madame Bourgeois is fed with fruit. She wakes up. She is pleased enough to tell Carlos: 'You know, this is not my first visit to Asia.'

At Ciego de Avila, in Camagüey, we stop off for lunch. Filling in a spare hour, Martha and I wander the quiet streets, meandering through the hot mid-day silence of a tropical town where all activity is taking place in cool rooms behind shuttered windows. Discovering us at large, a group of adolescent schoolgirls question us so far as language permits, allowing their shy eyes to dance over Martha's clothing only to the point where courtesy forbids. They smile, wish us good luck, and depart for their mid-day meal. We wander on, happy.

'Français?' We check our shuffle. Clearly the voice is directed at us but the source is not immediately apparent. When the sun is high the shadows are short and very sharp, so that there is no merging, no ambiguity of forms and spaces, only a chess-board of light and dark. As all spy novelists know, the see-er enjoys a great advantage over the seen, nor is this advantage peculiar to those situations where one must shoot or be shot. The advantage is also psychological ... like knowing a secret. It is a common mistake to believe that the *voyeur*, otherwise known as the Peeping Tom, is purely prurient in his motivation. He may well wish to see the lady naked; but at a distinctly more subconscious level he also needs the privilege of seeing without being seen, of establishing an identity by stealing an advantage. So the refusal of our interlocutor to reveal himself, to step out of the shadowed doorway, his greedy extension of that moment of privilege, already tells us something about him.

Three men in white shirts with short sleeves are standing in a doorway smoking cigars. Their hands are in their pockets.

'*Français?*' repeats the sleek, tubby one, and his hair is waved in oil. But he doesn't budge. A bell rings softly, uncertainly in my head; whatever his profession, this man is a pimp, his spiritual home is the big city where you 'stand off' when you accost a stranger, wary of the reaction, cards close to your chest, indifference elaborately assumed. I am immediately aware that these men are different: they will prove to be malcontents.

Martha says we are English. He is delighted to meet us and so too (he assures us, speaking on their behalf) are his two friends. He teaches English to an adult evening class and these are two of his best pupils and why don't we come along this evening to show how the language should be spoken and how a London accent sounds and are we married he sees we are he can always tell and he isn't married himself because he can't find a suitable girl in a one-horse town like this he only wishes he could get back to Havana where the action is where civilization is or was once (quickly slipped in to gauge our reaction) perhaps we can bring him

147

news from Havana have we been there? And what do we think of Cuba? he has relatives in Miami but he was ten at the time of the Revolution and stayed in Cuba with his grandmother and he hears that living standards have risen fast in Europe to speak only the truth he regards Europe as the cradle of civilization and he doesn't care for Latin Americans at all.

A short pause. It is still not clear to what extent his 'pupils' can follow his English.

'You don't like Latin Americans, then?'

'Not one bit, no, sir.'

'And you do not consider yourself one?'

'I have to, sir. They tell me I am one. Everyone in Cuba is now a Latin American but, pardon me, my father was from Spain and that's where I belong.'

'Where is he now—back in Spain?'

'In Pittsburgh, Pennsylvania. He sells insurance, sir, and is doing very well.'

'Would you like to join him there?'

'Sir, I know that in the Parliament of England every man speaks his mind but here in Cuba, sir, walls have ears.'

(Not, I think we would agree, the confession of a man notably afraid of being overheard.)

'But you don't feel happy in this town?'

'I don't. I am idle here. I am not idle by nature, sir. God gave me hands with which to work.'

'We understand that there has been a great effort to get teachers out of Havana into the provinces.'

'We have been told the same.' He assesses us. Tries to read us.

'And how have you found Cuba?' he asks.

'That's a big question.'

'Is Cuba what you expected—what you hoped to find?'

'Yes and no.'

'More yes or more no?'

'Certain things are very impressive.'

He nods, perhaps masking a certain disappointment.

'Of course,' he says, 'a tourist does not see everything a Cuban sees. You know, sir, there are some very unhappy people in Cuba today.'

'Are you one of them?'

'Sir, walls have ears.'

'Not English ears, surely.'

He laughs and translates this remark to his two companions; from which, and their intent silence, it emerges that his 'pupils' still have much English to learn. I ask him bluntly whether he would have preferred the old régime.

'Nowadays history is never the same.'

'I don't quite follow you.'

'From one day to the next, the past is rewritten. I have my own opinions. God made man to think for himself, sir. I assume you are both communicants of the High Anglican Church?'

I laugh. Martha laughs. He looks a little worried.

'You are good Communists, then?'

We both laugh.

'One must have a faith,' he says. 'Without a faith there is only materialism. Materialism, sir, is barren. It offers no hope neither to man nor beast nor fish nor fowl.'

When we bid him farewell his hands are still in his pockets.

In our hotel bedroom in Santa Clara we find a shiny green electric fan imported from Communist China. It works. After some consultation, we decide to reconnoitre the centre of the town before dinner. To reach the main square, says the hotel receptionist, you turn right, then left, then right again. Passing a Coppelia café whose pre-cast cement slabs are set at modernist angles, and whose long queue of expectant patrons stands placidly in the evening sunshine,

we reach the main square which is thronged with promen-
aders. How nice! How like a city! And how nice it would be
to settle down at an open-air table in front of a café, to sip a
Daiquiri, nibble an ice-cream, to watch the world walk by.
But the square is dominated by three imposing buildings:
a theatre in the Greek style, a tall hotel, where bullet holes
can still be seen on the upper storeys (Guevara took Santa
Clara on 29 December 1959 and Batista fled from Cuba three
days later), and a public library.

Well, that's an idea since we are both interested in books.
But does one need a reader's card or ticket to enter? We
pause hesitantly inside the door. The librarian glances up
and beckons us to enter, to have a look. The room is large,
but there are only about a dozen readers, most of them
students working at tables. Surveying the shelves, the first
thing one notices is that most of the books were published
a long time ago. Many of them are in English and some of
the newer ones in Russian. It remains to search for an
ideological pattern, to try and figure why so many books
published in America should remain on public library
shelves in a country which has developed such quick, confis-
catory reflexes. But there is no ideological pattern, no detect-
able purge of deviant and pernicious authors. I note down a
few names: Aristotle, Plato, Russell, Freud, Adler, Ortega y
Gasset, Schopenhauer, Husserl, Corliss Lamont, William
James, Piaget, Dewey, Hannah Arendt, Will Durant, Voltaire, Rousseau, Mauriac, Gide, Kierkegaard, Laski, Garaudy,
Paine, J. S. Mill, Alfred Marshall, Rosa Luxemburg, the
Webbs, Spengler, Churchill, Frank Harris, Gertrude Stein.
But nothing written by any foreign author about Revolu-
tionary Cuba. That is a different ball-game.

We are on the verge of leaving when the librarian, a man
in his late thirties or early forties, who has been regarding us
sidelong with obvious curiosity, moves in our direction.

'Français?'

'*Anglais.*'

'Ah, good. We don't see many English people here. Santa Clara has only recently come on to the tourist map.'

'You speak excellent English.'

'Thank you. I studied at Yale for two years.'

'When was that?'

'Before the Revolution, of course.' He smiles. 'We don't send so many of our students to Yale now.'

'Maybe one day ...'

'Oh yes ...'

Martha remarks that the library has an interesting collection of books.

'Most of them are out of date. We have to make do with what we have. For example, I would like very much to have some of the latest novels from England. But ...' he shrugs, 'first things first.'

He asks us where we have been in Cuba and what are our impressions.

'Well ...'

'Please speak your mind. I shall not take offence.'

'People have great self-confidence and dignity here.'

'Yes, of course.'

I sense that he is impatient with courtesies and is thirsting to answer criticisms which he can very well anticipate.

'The Cuban Press is lousy,' I say.

'Lousy? Why so?'

'It all comes out of one mouth.'

'In a society like ours, you see, there is agreement on certain fundamentals. They pass beyond the area of debate. But you should not imagine that nothing is debated here in Cuba. Fidel Castro positively encourages discussion, you know.'

'Is it healthy for a country, a people, to be so dominated by one man?'

'Dominated is not the word I would choose. Did Churchill

dominate the British people during the war—or did he simply express their cause better than anyone else?'

'At the end of the war they were free to throw him out.'

'Believe me, if Fidel ever thought the Cuban people didn't need him any more, he would go and live in the country.'

I ask the librarian whether he is able to obtain foreign newspapers.

'Irregular. Sometimes. Whenever I open one I read that Fidel is suffering from a mortal illness.'

'I see you have quite a wide range of Soviet books and periodicals.'

'Yes, we have. Mostly technical and scientific.'

'Can many people read Russian?'

'Not the older generation. But the young people learn it in school. And of course we now have many students who have studied in the Soviet Union.'

'Do you feel writers and artists enjoy enough intellectual freedom in Cuba?'

He reflects on this.

'Who is to judge what is enough?—that is the problem. In every revolution certain strains develop. They require tact and understanding on both sides.'

I tell him about the confiscation of our books at the airport. He seems surprised, and a few moments later politely excuses himself.

There is still time to kill before dinner so we wander into a small shop where sets of postage stamps are displayed in colourful cellophane packets. Choosing a couple of packets, we advance on the lady assistant.

'*Cuanto, por favor?*'

Of course, just as a little learning is proverbially a dangerous thing, so are a few words of a foreign language. Misleading, they invite the torrential discourse which we, completely uncomprehending, now suffer. But it generally emerges that no, we can't buy these stamps, nor *these* there (a smiling shake of the head), nor *those* (shake). The more she refuses, the more helpful and friendly our assistant becomes: it's all rather Chinese. We depart carrying some stamps we didn't particularly want, leaving behind us a lady wreathed in smiles.

The green and pleasant campus of the University of Santa Clara reminds me more of Sussex University than of Stonybrook. Now equipped with new laboratories and a large amphitheatre with raked seats, Santa Clara University was founded in 1952, mainly to act as a stabilizing counterweight to the radicalism of Havana and Santiago Universities. Since 1959, the number of students enrolled at Santa Clara has increased from seven hundred to more than four thousand, and all of these students receive not only their education, but also their accommodation, free (except those whose families live in Santa Clara). Five new faculties have been added to those of Science and the Humanities: they are Technology, Medicine, Agriculture, Economics, and Pedagogy. Each faculty is subdivided into a number of schools. The Technology faculty, for example, includes the schools of Mechanics, Chemistry, Electronics, and Industry. Production-oriented studies are the ones encouraged: isolated or esoteric research is out of favour.

The régime has increased the universities from three to six, the teaching contingent from 1,053 to 4,449 (in 1970), and the number of full-time students from 25,000 to 40,000 (in 1969). Students attending technical schools have multiplied fivefold. In 1969 fifteen million books were produced, mainly textbooks, many of them translated from the Russian, and about seventy per cent of them were distributed free.

Male students spend fifteen days a year in a military camp and also serve in the militia during the week. Girls do rifle practice. All curricula involve a year's course in dialectical materialism.

Cuban universities are not, as in the West, hotbeds of dissent. They are not permitted to be. The Minister of Education, José Llanusa, remarked: 'We shall not have a Czechoslovakia here.' In 1960 the autonomy of Havana University was subverted from within and destroyed. Two-thirds of the teaching staff were dismissed and a Communist, Dr Juan Marinello, was appointed Rector. Inexorably, all forms of unorthodoxy and individualism were weeded out, culminating in a new purge in 1964-65. Nor was political nonconformism the only target. Fidel launched a cultural revolution of his own, directed against homosexuals, long hair, fancy clothes, pop music, drugs, short skirts, 'imperialist jukeboxes', and anything which made life worth living for the young. In 1968 the hippie cult was squashed.

Castro has on occasion warned against a facile conformism. In March 1962, in a speech at Havana University, he asked: 'Do we, perhaps, want a youth which will simply limit itself to listening and parroting what we say? No! We want a youth which will think.' He then castigated a student who had spoken in commemoration of José Antonio Echevarría (killed in 1957) but who, in quoting Echevarría, had studiously omitted a reference to God. Castro was outraged: '*Compañeros*, could we be so cowardly ... so intellectually warped ... so morally wretched, as to suppress these lines?' Were Martí's words to be suppressed because he too was not a Marxist-Leninist? No, said Castro, 'the Revolution must be a school of unfettered thought.' And he went out of his way to condemn the slogan, apparently popular among the Rebel Youth, 'We are socialists, forward, forward, and whoever doesn't like it let him take a laxative!' (Who are you going to win over with that?)

All this reminds me of what an East German professor once told me in defence of his régime: 'There is no cult of personality here! Why, Walter Ulbricht himself has condemned it many times!'

In short, only the Personality is in a position to condemn his Cult. When Castro calls for unfettered thought, there is unfettered thought. But when he grows impatient with the wrong kind of unfettered thought, then it is fettered again. A country like Cuba is almost inevitably caught in rhetorical contradictions. Says Castro: 'The people have become Marxists out of conviction; because the Revolution itself has convinced them.' But it hasn't convinced them enough, so—he continues—the time will come when young people will acquire 'that true Revolutionary spirit, that profound conviction' by studying Marxism for eight years, from junior high-school to university.

At Santa Clara the Dean of Students welcomes us and declares himself to be at our disposal. He will be glad to answer questions on any topic. Short-haired, tanned, strong-jawed, and wearing no tie, he reminds me of a Californian swimming coach who is confident that his team will lift all the medals before the season is out. The Dean's team is not only Santiago but also Cuba. Yes, he enjoys considerable responsibility and, if we insist on the word, power, being directly responsible to the Rector who is chosen by the Minister of Education. (I am still searching Cuba for an example of a collegiate-autonomous process of decision.)

For a while Nicole asks congratulatory questions to which she knows the answers, the effect being rather like an interview of the President of the United States conducted by his Press Secretary. Sensing that time is running out (the Dean has begun to glance at a formidable watch which is obviously water-proof, shock-proof, and doubt-proof), I am forced, when my own moment comes, to eschew those preliminary questions which might disarm suspicion.

'What proportion of the pre-1959 faculty now remains at Santa Clara?'

'Thirty per cent.'

'That's a big turn-over.'

155

'Yes. Most of the thirty per cent are scientific and technical staff.'

'So there was a clean sweep in the Humanities?'

'Many of the old professors could not come to terms with the Revolution. They were politicians in spirit, élitist and privileged ... individualists, egoists.'

'What has become of them?'

'They have gone to the United States where they belong.'

'May I ask how textbooks are chosen?'

'Yes. There is no censorship. The aim is to expose imperialist propaganda not to ban it.'

'Are there differences of opinion among the staff?'

'Of course.'

'On political questions?'

'No, none at all.'

'Even where political questions touch philosophical ones?'

'On such subjects there are discussions. But we believe that there is only one form of Marxism-Leninism, even though there are erroneous interpretations of it.'

'Do students have the right to criticize their professors?'

'In what sense?'

The Dean plays with a pipe which he occasionally lights, lets go out, then lays on the table top. He has a box of matches. A few moments ago his competent fingers were caressing it gently; now the box is bouncing fiercely from hand to hand.

'In the sense of being able to record whether they are well taught.'

'Certainly. But no "liberalist" criticism is allowed.'

'What does that mean?'

The Dean does not answer directly. He says that student opinion is voiced through the Federation of Students—where there are discussions. 'I understand that the Federation has been merged with the Young Communist League?'

'The word merged is not correct.'

'I realize that your time is valuable, but may I ask you about art and literature?'

'Yes, of course. Any question. I said so, at the beginning.'

'In recent years there have been some literary disputes in Cuba.' (The Dean regards me warily, refusing to be drawn.) 'I mean disputes about the proper content and form of socialist literature. Are such disputes the subject of active controversy within the University?'

'No one dictates to our writers.'

Pause.

'Perhaps you misunderstood my question in translation?'

Carlos begins to retranslate, but the Dean indicates with an impatient gesture that he understood perfectly. The matchbox rattles.

'Did you have something in mind?' he asks me.

'The Padilla case for example.'*

'Padilla was criticized for the reactionary content of his poems.'

'Do the students here debate such issues?'

'Naturally. The Federation of Students passed a resolution.'

'Was there any measure of disagreement among them?'

'The resolution was unanimous.'

'May I ask you this: do you believe a poet may legitimately write simply to please himself?'

'It would be anti-social.'

'Who can judge the social value of abstract art?'

The Dean's eyes blaze with anger now. He is distempered not so much (I guess) by my persistence, my dog-with-bone behaviour, as by a single phrase: 'Who can judge?' One notion above all others is odious to the Overseer—that opinions are merely opinions. It is no good trying to explain to him that he and his kind are repeating the mistake made by the Catholic Inquisition when it enjoyed a monopoly of

* See pages 160 and 164.

power in Europe; to remind him that history repeats itself
down to the most elementary errors would be also to imply
that history will bury him. Without honour.

I could make out a case for the Dean. The Western
democracies have never enjoyed, or even recommended,
absolute freedom of opinion. The First Amendment as interpreted by the United States Supreme Court demonstrates
how a splendid principle (free speech, etc.) has to be qualified by the pressure of circumstances. In America, Communists were sent to jail not for doing something but
(purportedly) for advocating doing something, the argument
being that advocacy leads to incitement and that any social
system is entitled to defuse bombs before they explode. The
Dean of Santa Clara would also point out (if he had time,
but his watch now dominates the proceedings) that neither
American Governments nor American public opinion
display notable concern when censorship is practised by
right-wing dictatorships in Latin America. Jefferson is held
up as a model to all the world only when the natives start
filching private property and upsetting United Fruit.

Nevertheless, I cannot make out a very convincing case
for the Dean. It is a long haul from panicked incursions on
freedom of opinion in times of war or stress to the insistence
that there is only one true philosophy of history and that all
individual behaviour must conform to it. Human beings are
not naturally tolerant. A tradition of tolerance is largely
the delicate, frail, precarious cultivation of visionary minds
whose enlightened attitudes take root in societies where
rapid economic progress has imposed a spirit of compromise
on rival social classes, none of whom can any longer make
good a claim to total dominance. But once that equilibrium is
upset, and once the leadership cadres ignore or reject the
vital wisdom of Milton, Voltaire, Jefferson and Mill, that the
human mind progresses through the free interchange of
ideas, and that truth must conquer untruth in equal battle in

order to be truth—once this wisdom is jettisoned, liberty can be uprooted within hours. And when a single doctrine or dogma gains ascendancy, the claim to supremacy is registered not by the doctrine but by its human salesmen and beneficiaries. When the Dean tells us that philosophy has finally culminated in a single living Truth, Marxism-Leninism, he is giving notice that we have entered the throne room on sufferance and had better wipe our feet. Once entrenched, the new élite, the guardians of Truth, become increasingly suspicious of whispered dissent, of veiled dissent, of concealed dissent; paranoid by virtue of their usurpation, they lay relentless siege to that one fortress of sedition which refuses to capitulate, to yield up its garrison —the human mind. The silent motions behind a man's placid gaze fill them with foreboding; tormented by suspicion, they demand of him ever more elaborate professions of loyalty and proofs of virtue.

The impact of such a climate on art and literature need not be guessed at. We have enough examples at hand to know the inevitable outcome. When every dissenter has been tamed, subdued, or eliminated, there still remains the terrible possibility that the contagion may be carried on the printed page, passed from hand to hand and silently absorbed. This is why our books were confiscated at José Martí Airport. Inoculation! When the interior has been subdued, the infiltration of foreign ideas assumes a menace out of all proportion to the reality.

Two foreign writers have particularly enraged Castro, the more so that they are socialists and, as such, had been welcomed in Cuba at an official level. One of them is the veteran French agronomist René Dumont, who, frequently employed as a consultant by Third World régimes, was first summoned to Revolutionary Cuba in 1960. His last meeting with Castro took place in June 1969 and is described by Dumont as 'somewhat tumultuous', with the Cuban leader angrily challenging Dumont's hypercritical attitude towards the Soviet Union and accusing him of harbouring a European superiority complex. On leaving Cuba, Dumont published a book significantly titled *Cuba est-il socialiste?* (Is Cuba Socialist?). Arguing that collectivized property, economic planning, and the priority of collective needs do not in themselves constitute authentic socialism, Dumont calls for greater self-management in the factories, more liberty of information, and a greater tolerance of divergent opinions in Cuba. Harsh in many of his judgments, he estimates that twenty-five to thirty per cent of Havana's population would depart tomorrow for the United States if it were free to do so. Not one of Dumont's three reports on Cuba has been published there.

The other offender is the experienced and widely travelled journalist K. S. Karol, whose basic sympathy for socialist systems has never blunted his critical independence. His book, *Guerrillas in Power* (1970), written after an extended visit to Cuba and several long interviews with Castro, was obviously regarded by Fidel as a vile betrayal. In Karol's view, the Cuban people deserve more initiative, more self-determination, and more immunity from the arbitrary manipulations of a remote bureaucracy. But Karol's most biting comments strike at Castro's unqualified support for Soviet foreign policy since the resubjugation of Czechoslovakia in August 1968, his betrayal of his sympathizers in Mexico, and his determination to retain total personal control of every aspect of Cuban life.

On top of this, the Padilla case* generated formidable protests from many distinguished foreign intellectuals (notably Sartre and Simone de Beauvoir), who had hitherto been counted among Cuba's most ardent supporters. Once again the international Left found itself in the divorce court. Castro's reaction was characteristic of the man. What do they know?

* See page 164.

Who do they think they are? They came, they saw, they said kind things, but really they understood nothing. To hell with them. We don't need them here. Nor their books. Give instructions to the customs officers that in future ...

At lunch one day we discuss the issue with Carlos. He is aware that certain foreign visitors have returned to their own countries and subsequently 'betrayed' Cuban hospitality, but he is genuinely in ignorance of their names.

'But when Russians visit America or Britain they return home and write critical reports,' I object.

'Yes, of course.'

'Does that amount to a betrayal of hospitality?'

'They would not be welcome a second time.'

'Do you feel that foreign critics are a danger to Cuba?'

'They may mislead ignorant people.'

'Can ignorant people read English, French, or Dutch?'

Carlos shrugs. 'Each country must work out its own road of development. One should not interfere in other people's affairs.'

'What was Guevara doing in Bolivia, then? He was not a Bolivian.'

'That is a question of Latin American solidarity. The European intellectuals do not enjoy any solidarity with the people of Cuba.'

I think this is true. But they do, of course, enjoy some solidarity with the intellectuals of Cuba, and with some students also, many of whom have in recent years lapsed into a helpless despondency. Here I must take an encounter out of geographical and chronological context: on a 'free' afternoon in a certain town we make a rendezvous with a Cuban writer who, let us imagine, is a friend of a friend of mine. He does not invite us to his apartment, and cafés are hopeless, so we meet at the foot of a conspicuous monument in a central square and we take a walk. I present him with a couple of my own books, which he accepts very graciously, regretting that he cannot return the compliment since, his present situation being what it is, the discovery of his books in our baggage would do him no good. (They are no longer available in bookshops.)

In the early years of the Revolution his work was much praised and prizes came his way. Sent abroad on delegations and as a journalist, he was generally encouraged to make contact with foreign intellectuals. In recent times, however, along with certain colleagues of like mind, he has fallen under a cloud. His teaching job in a university faculty of literature was the first victim of this displeasure; then he was removed from the editorial board of a magazine; finally his books disappeared from the bookstores and it was made clear to him that he could no longer expect to earn a living from writing. He now works in quite a humble capacity on a development project. This experience, he says, is fascinating : he only wishes he could write about it!

Antonio (as I shall call him) has been a dedicated supporter of the Revolution from its earliest days. He regrets nothing, nor does he disown his commitment; he is, however, sadly convinced that in its middle echelons the Revolution has fallen into the hands of philistines, mediocrities, and opportunists. I ask him whether his attitude does not resemble that of the nineteenth-century Russian peasants who attributed all their sufferings to the local gentry, but remained convinced that the 'little father' in Petersburg, the Tsar, would alleviate their misery if only he knew about it. Antonio laughs at this, then stops laughing. Man of the world though he is, he finds it almost impossible to criticize Fidel or to contemplate the possibility that the head really wags the uglier tail of the dog. He remembers Fidel saying, in June 1961 : 'There can be, of course, artists, and good artists, who do not have a revolutionary attitude towards life, and it is precisely for that group of artists and intellectuals that the Revolution constitutes a problem.'

Castro went out of his way to reassure them that Cuba would not imitate Soviet cultural policy or impose the aesthetic principles of socialist realism. 'What principles of expression should the artist follow in his effort to reach the people? What should the people demand from the artist? Can we make a general statement about this? No, it would be over-simplified.'

Antonio remembers these words and I too recall the gist of them—how warmly they were received abroad!—with their refreshing promise of a new partnership between the political and artistic avant-gardes. At that time even 'counter-revolutionary' works could still be obtained in bookstores, and no creative writer felt anything but free to do his own thing. Then the foreign periodicals began to vanish; next, in August 1961, the Union of Artists and Writers was formed under the presidency of the sixty-year-old black Communist poet, Nicolás Guillén, former typographer, journalist, diplomat, and civil servant, veteran of the Spanish Civil War and of many Communist Peace Congresses. Guillén now became the 'national poet'; ten years later, on the occasion of his seventieth birthday, he was awarded the Soviet Order of the Red Flag of Labour. Thus, from 1961, Cuban writers had extended to them the model of the 'good poet', the poet whose attitudes should be emulated. Denunciations of individualism, ivory-towerism, and pure poetry gained momentum. Listen, for example, to Félix Pita Rodríguez in his 'Chronicles of a New Dawn':

> Poets who cry out their solitude
> Enthroned on marble pedestals
> Decorated with cornucopias,
>
> ...
>
> All is treason which is not
> Poetry with a purpose.*

* Translated by Claudia Beck.

And he adds that his own is 'poetry with a purpose, desperately dedicated'. I find these sentiments extremely ugly. In a Communist society it is not typically the solitary poets who are enthroned on marble pedestals, but rather the Nicolás Guilléns and the politicians who patronize them. The solitary poets cry out somewhere else and continue to cry out until their corpses have been rehabilitated. Cuba has not committed such atrocities, but the writer who speaks of 'treason' in this context is encouraging a witch-hunt.

The Cultural Congress of Havana, held in January 1968, was the last attempt to reconcile Revolutionary discipline with the liberal sensibilities of foreign sympathizers. Many foreign delegates departed full of admiration for Cuba's experimental films, architecture, and music, for the prizes and bursaries distributed to Latin American writers by La Casa de las Américas, and generally for a tolerant cultural climate held to be unique among revolutionary régimes.

In October 1968 an international jury appointed by the Union of Writers and Artists awarded its poetry prize to Heberto Padilla and its drama prize to Antón Arrufat. But when their prize-winning works were published a critical preface was included, and quite suddenly the Army periodical *Verde Olivo* launched an attack on these two writers, characterizing them as malcontents who had exploited the licence of art to denigrate the Revolution. This bitter tirade was echoed in *Granma*. At a stroke Padilla, a poet and reporter previously held in high regard, and for a time the chief London correspondent of the news agency Prensa Latina, was silenced. Having dared to complain of a stifling cultural atmosphere, he proved his point the hard way.

But Guillén continues to be honoured, the implacable critic of America:

I, Juan, Negro,

I have the land and the sea,
no country-club,
no high-life,
no tennis club,
no yacht,
Nothing but beach to beach, wave to wave,
Gigantic blue open free
In short, the sea.*

In another poem, 'Way Back When', he further reflects
on America's passing cultural dominance:

How great! Cincinnati beat Pittsburgh
And St Louis beat Detroit
(Buy Reich-brand baseballs, they're the best),
We modeled our boxing champions
After Jack Johnson.
. . .
Nothing better than Walk-Over Shoes
And Dr Ross' pills.
. . .
We chose them as our mentors
So that our elections would be fast and undisputed
. . .
So that the Whites would not mingle with Negroes
So that we could chew chewing-gum,
. . .
So that there would never be a revolution,
So that we could pull the chain of the water-closet,
Just once, and hard.
But it happened
That one day we saw ourselves as children grown
Who discover that the venerable uncle who sat
    them on his knees

* Translated by Lenox and Maryanne Raphael.

165

Has been jailed for forgery ...*

This poem is here presented in translation and considerations of space have led me to cut passages where indicated. As poetry, as a work of art, we therefore should not judge it, merely taking note of the spirit behind it: polemical, astringent, public. Now let us listen to Heberto Padilla's 'The Childhood of William Blake':

But through the shuttered window,
He hears the seed-pod tick against the tree,
As though somebody were rapping.
His most secret game has grown in craftiness.
Disconsolate he sees, across the darkened plain,
The rising smoke from the houses burning in the
   night
And animals passing against the flame.
Don't open the door. Don't call.
...
Any day now
They'll burst into my room—
He showed his badge, sir.
Any day now
They'll force me out onto the street,
Beating me, battering me about
As though I were a sewer rat.
(You cannot understand this. It is of our time.)
The inspector of heresies will testify against me.

Antonio knows these lines by heart. He recites them in Spanish, thanks me again for my humble gift, and shakes

* Translated by Anita Whitney Romeo.

our hands. Probably I shall never know what he thought of my books.

But enough of this gloom! Cuba is a holiday, Cuba is the sun, and we are now arriving at a seaside paradise, the resort of Varadero. Broad white sands, palm trees, swimming-pools, and the villas of millionaires stretch along the shore in luxuriant space. Varadero is a slender finger-peninsula of pleasure jutting out into the sea on the north coast, and Monsieur Lepinay has already stripped down and offered up his panting brown flesh to his god. Europeans come here in the late summer, Canadians in the winter, and Cuban families all the year round. Even after political independence, the natives of the West Indian islands are still barred from long expanses of their own coastline, whose owner is the White Moloch. A man who cannot take his family down to the sea on Sunday is scarcely living in his own country; large automobiles sweep past him, white arms hanging lazily, arrogantly out of the windows as if to challenge him: 'Do without our wealth if you can.' Castro accepted the challenge and did without the wealth, opening the old Havana Biltmore Yacht Club to the public at a price of fifty cents, seizing the mansions of Varadero and opening the Intercontinental to Cuban families at prices they could easily afford. A week's vacation for a whole family costs only fifteen dollars.

We find ourselves in the most elegant of bedrooms— 'Regency' fabrics, tall french windows, a marble-floored bathroom, spacious mosquito nets, chests inlaid with fine woods. Beyond the windows, the sighing sea. We decide to remain here for the rest of our lives and, thus decided, hire Russian bicycles (the sort where you have to back-pedal in order to brake) for a peso each, and set out to explore, delighted to be our own engines. The ride is bumpy because the lady who offered us forty two-wheelers from which to choose could not find a single pump with which to inflate any of the eighty wheels. Along the way we stop to watch a scratch game of baseball, impressively skilled and fiercely competitive, but I have to decline when I am invited to balance the teams. We return to our 'hotel', a mansion once owned by a Cuban tobacco king and graced with a swimming-pool, table-tennis, chess-sets, a bar, and a restaurant of genuine elegance. This we enter in our best clothes, taking our places at any time of our choosing at separate tables laid with starched covers and heavy silver cutlery.

On this excessively humid evening I at last trap Carlos into a second game of chess. (Meanwhile, over there, nice Spassky has returned to Moscow to face the music.) Martha sits beside our table and watches for two trembling hours of grunting, sighing, and cigarette-lighting, sweetly accepting the Cuban myth that chess is a matter of muscle and *machismo*. (I assume that a Cuban male beaten at chess by a woman would accelerate his cherished rendezvous with death.) Carlos's style is leopard-like; crouching over the board, he emanates a feline intensity, then leaps, moving his piece with terrible *aplomb* and banging it down as if to say, 'wriggle out of that if you can!' I wriggle. Desperate notions of honour sharpen my normally slack and careless game: Don't make a simple mistake! Concentration is half the battle, and a steel band of fire is splitting my skull, but Carlos Capablanca falters in the face of a late queen's-side attack, he needs an extra pawn in defence, he resigns. We shake hands, and rivers of sweat are exchanged in the act. It is well past midnight.

The next day, pausing at a nearby house formerly owned by Batista, with an underground passage leading to its once-private beach, we make tracks for a vast Xanadu-like mansion built in the bad old days by René Du Pont and nationalized in 1964. It cost a hundred thousand dollars, possesses its own golf course, and was once protected from intruders by seventy-five hired retainers. Walled and pillared in Italian marble, stocked with English Wedgwood pottery carrying the same ivy pattern used by Napoleon on St Helena, and boasting the most gorgeous wooden ceilings, the mansion rises to an open dancing-floor, level with a roof of green tiles imported from Boston. Well, well: we gape and probe and confidently pace the floor-blocks painted in goat's milk. The family photo-albums reveal among other things a passion for pet iguanas, which the Du Ponts enjoyed persuading to leap, dance, fight, and make love on the lawn. Now preserved as a museum, the house also accommodates conferences and vacationing *'Moncadianos'*—workers who have outstripped their colleagues in zeal and efficiency. (I suppose René Du Pont, in his more pretentious way, did just that.) I must report that some of the French ladies are getting extremely excited, though for different reasons: Madame Bourgeois is more awake than at any time since her arrival in Cuba, and I wouldn't be surprised if one or two choice items of Wedgwood didn't accompany her back to France; but little plump Madame Lepinay, daughter of toil, is cueing her sisters into a new chorus of anti-Americanism, and I am forced to endure renewed denunciations of the British Royal Family whose many privileges and palaces—Madame Lepinay insists—should promptly be turned over to British *Moncadianos*.

That evening torrential rain falls. The electricity fails. We rush to close and fasten our french windows. The wind shrieks and a tornado rips across the coastline a mile to our west. In the morning, when all is calm and sunshine, Carlos takes us to see the result: a neat corridor only one hundred yards wide in which every building has been ripped from its foundations and hurled to the ground. But on either side of the corridor not a tile has been displaced. We take pictures.

Close to Varadero lies Boca de Camarioca, a short stretch

of deserted coast with an aeroplane runway reserved for the export of a Cuban breed known as the *gusano*, or 'worm'. A *gusano* is he who chooses to emigrate. Since December 1965 a regular service has lifted three or four thousand émigrés a month in airliners chartered by the American Government. The decision to leave, which must be registered at least six months ahead of the intended date of departure, involves an immediate loss of employment and systematic ostracism. Almost all possessions have to be left behind and, once the plane is airborne, the decision is irreversible—it's a one-way ticket. Not everyone is free to leave at even so inhibiting a price: most males aged between fifteen and twenty-seven are obliged to remain—even if it means splitting the family—as are certain categories of technicians and skilled workers.

'You ask me why I don't emigrate,' Antonio has said. 'I ask myself that almost every week. The truth is, I have always despised the *gusanos*, and there is a part of me which says: you have your reasons and they had their reasons and when you meet up with them in Miami your reasons will become their reasons. You will be a *gusano* too.'

Yet a country of seven million people has in just over a decade lost more than half a million to the emigration. Proportionally, one must imagine fifteen million Americans quitting their country, bitter, dispossessed, consumed by a sense of betrayal.

The first to scramble, naturally enough, were Batista's top henchmen. Their planes groaned into the sky, loaded with loot. Then went the frightened rich. By the end of 1960, following the expropriations, rent laws, and purges of the Press, universities, schools and trade unions, Cubans were flooding into Florida. Some of them were skilled and semi-skilled workers. In Washington, the Senate Internal Security Sub-Committee carefully selected from this exodus the witnesses it judged most friendly: for example, former Chief of Staff Tabernilla. With American encouragement (officially denied), exiles began to fly bombing missions from Florida, striking at sugar mills, harbours, and town centres. Meanwhile, internal sabotage rose to dangerous levels in 1960.

As executions mounted within Cuba, disillusioned members of the 26 July Movement began to take flight along with the intimidated bourgeoisie. Miró Cardona, Prime Minister until February 1959; President Urrutia, appointed by Fidel, then sacked by Fidel after warning against the growth of Communist influence; Manuel Ray, former Minister of Public Works—they all departed. Two émigré organizations, the MRR and the MRP, intensified the campaign of terrorism, fires, explosions, and derailments, striking at oil-refineries and warehouses. The most popular radio commentator of the Revolution and a violent opponent of *Yanqui* imperialism, Pardo Llada, fled to Mexico in March 1961, complaining that his freedom had been eliminated by Communists. Another popular radio commentator and a friend of Castro's, Conte Agüero, also voiced fears of a Communist takeover, was immediately attacked in the Press, and took flight. Some were unlucky: David Salvador, formerly Secretary-General of the Trade Union Movement, was captured while trying to escape in a yacht, brought to trial, and imprisoned.

The fact is that the emigration spans a wide spectrum of human types and social motives. No single judgment could cover them all. One type is cleverly depicted in 'Witness for the Prosecution', a poem by Luis Suardíaz, who in 1962 was appointed Director of Literature of the National Council of Culture:

> Every day at a quarter to three,
> She would enter the Dime Store cafeteria,
> Place her elbows delicately
> On the shiny counter of formica,

As though it were a precious piece of crystal,
Order her ice cream, vanilla,
An ice cold Coca Cola with a straw,
Syrup and a great big wedge of cake.

...

She worked in the office of a foreign concern,
Lived in a two-storey house without a garden.
She had studied to be a teacher,
And then was probably about 23 years old.
I believe she left about 1961.

...

I liked to observe her, since she was
A symbol of the mechanical life
Of a certain social type
Who consumes an expensive snack
At a quarter to three every afternoon.

...

Would she be likely to put up
With voluntary work, queues, ration books,
A possible shortage of chocolate cake?...*

Yes, as the poet says, she is 'incapable of the slightest sacrifice', and we all have to wonder what degree of sacrifice, of disruption, of deprivation, would seem to us not so slight. For more than fifty years large segments of Cuban urban society were enthralled by American affluence and American opportunity; such people are patriotic only in the sentimental sense and their love-of-country tends to evaporate when the supply of cheap domestic servants runs dry. But our poet does not tell the whole story, and if his chocolate-cake girl is typical, so also are the many genuine democrats who despaired at the inexorable erosion of a liberty once so loudly promised.

* Translated by Claudia Beck.

We are on the move again, but reluctantly. Everyone loves Varadero. Monsieur Lepinay registers a formal request to be allowed to stay there for the remainder of the holiday but is politely refused; he must continue with the package. Meanwhile, the Old Swiss, plunging in and out of the sea with many a wondrous imprecation, has seen his second shirt dried by the sun and confided to me that back in Switzerland his father still sends him to bed at ten o'clock. Because of which, or despite which—I am not sure—he wishes to guillotine the rich the world over. His ventriloquist's imitation of a falling guillotine would have made the Scarlet Pimpernel tremble.

Further up the coast we come to Jibacoa where the burnished young gods and goddesses who accompanied us from Prague have been doing heaven knows what in little concrete huts set between the trees, snorkelling, skin-diving, surfing, lying in hammocks, lizarding in the sun round the bar, and generally toasting their gorgeous limbs to peaks of indescribable sensuality. Madame Bourgeois, finding here a first-class boutique, runs amok and has to be carried back to the coach epileptic with frustration.

Now forget Varadero, forget Jibacoa, we are once again crossing the island to the south coast with serious intent. Passing through an empty countryside of marshes, swamps, and thick forests, we finally arrive at the Playa Girón sector of the Bahía de Cochinos—the Bay of Pigs. This is a pilgrimage, for it was here, in April 1961, that President Kennedy reaped the consequences of the most disastrous adventure of his career, the abortive attempt to overthrow Castro by force. (Please understand: North America has never saved the soul of a Latin American country.)

Once again we must embroil ourselves in that inescapable if painful topic—the enmity which simmers between Cuba and the United States. To begin with, there was a flirtation if not a honeymoon; visiting America in April 1959, Castro uttered enough anti-Communist remarks to reassure the public, if not Vice-President Nixon, who, after a discussion with Castro, advised Eisenhower to put him down quickly. The President heeded his advice to the point of ordering the training and equipping of Cuban refugees in March 1960. By May, American officers were running training camps for exiled Cubans on Guatemala's Pacific coast. It was at this time that Secretary of State Herter asked innocently why 'the voter of the Americas' (a rare animal) should ever 'willingly enslave himself to a monolithic economy, surrender his individual freedom ... or relegate himself to the status of a landless servitor to a new bureaucratic aristocracy'. Whether Herter felt that these words bore any relevance to Batista's Cuba we may never know. But when Cuba expropriated that economic monolith worth eight hundred million dollars, the Telephone Company, and relieved Cuba's landless servitors of the obligation to work on three million acres of American-owned land, both Herter and Eisenhower felt that a white man's patience has its limits. (The Canadian Government under Conservative Premier Diefenbaker refused to join the American embargo, with the sweet result that expropriated Canadian banks were compensated in cash.)

In September 1960 Castro conducted with boisterous bravado his invasion of Manhattan, embracing Khrushchev, rocking the United Nations, and generally offering American citizens a much-needed lesson in what it is like to entertain unwelcome visitors. Meanwhile Guevara was portrayed on the cover of *Time* in ogre-ish colours and the *Washington Post* spoke of 'the Charles Addamsish Rasputin of the Revolution, Maj. Ernesto "Che" Guevara...' Two American writers, Robert Scheer and Maurice Zeitlin, have studied every article about Cuba published during the first twenty-two months of the Revolutionary régime in *Life, Time, Newsweek, US News and World Report, Reader's Digest,*

Look, Saturday Evening Post, and *Coronet*—a total of two hundred and twenty-one articles. 'What we found in each magazine offered an excellent subject for the study, not of the Cuban revolution, but rather of propaganda ... in the worst sense of the term.' Positive social or economic achievements were ignored or, if mentioned, accompanied by scare-phrases about 'soaking the rich'. Cubans were being 'herded' into 'mass institutions'.

Kennedy inherited Eisenhower's invasion plan and did not long delay its implementation. The aim was to establish a beach-head secure enough to fly in the Cuban Revolutionary Council, which would in turn call for full-scale American military aid. But the military operation aborted. When 1,297 US-trained and equipped invaders landed on 15 April, Castro's small airforce had not been destroyed and proceeded to make havoc of the supply and support ships, the result being that 1,180 prisoners were taken, publicly tried on television, and only released in return for medical and other supplies worth fifty-seven million dollars. But the invasion also precipitated a great purge within Cuba, the arrest of at least 100,000 people by the militia, including all the Catholic bishops, many journalists and the greater part of the counter-revolutionary underground, of whom an estimated 2,500 were agents of the CIA.

Miró Cardona, head of the Cuban Revolutionary Council in exile, had several subsequent meetings with President Kennedy, on each occasion coming away with the impression that a military solution was still contemplated, and in December 1962 Kennedy told veterans of the Bay of Pigs that Cuba would be liberated by force of arms.

Here the Cuban poet Samuel Feijóo puts the other side of the story in his poem 'Trip to the Trenches':

> The militiamen of my town who were killed by the
> invader

Were shoemakers,
Bricklayers,
Musicians and canecutters. Their mothers
Were my mothers.
                    Hatred
Murdered them.
...
What does it matter to them
If a million Cuban peasants
Perish? These are not the ones who worship the
    dollar.
Like the Japanese at Hiroshima, they are
Inferior.*

Here, perhaps, a good case is marred by sentimental rhetoric; 'mothers' usually do more harm than good to poetic lamentations for war.

Next came the Missile Crisis. A large military force was massed in Florida and military leaders called for air strikes and an invasion, but Kennedy played a statesman's role and quite possibly saved the world from nuclear war by affording Khrushchev the time and scope to withdraw his missiles from Cuban territory. Soon afterwards, Russia and the United States made progress towards a global rapprochement and Cuba became the implicit beneficiary of a wider package-deal. Henceforward, the White House classified Castro as a bearable thorn in the flesh, hoped he would succumb to internal erosion, and allowed the CIA to play roulette with Havana. But for Cuban Davids the Goliath called Les Estados Unidos remained uncomfortably menacing: as José Alvarez Baragano put it, 'In the Pentagon':

I hear them behind glass walls
In refrigerated air

* Translated by Angela Boyer.

Exhaling blasts of gangrene and gunpowder
Measuring our steps
Calculating our weight
Filing us by number and description
...
But we are beyond their calculations.*

At Playa Girón we disembark. Outside a new fishing college a crowd of lads in white shirts is happily idling in the sun. The museum itself proves to be closed and Carlos disappears on one of his customary expeditions to trace the key. Meanwhile, we examine a captured Sherman tank and part of a propeller-driven plane. Carlos returns triumphant with the key. On entering the museum we are assaulted by swarms of venomous mosquitoes who force us to retreat in disorder, wildly slapping at expanses of exposed skin. My wife and I, prudent as ever, have just enough cream to layer ourselves, and this time the Young Swiss is out of luck since he never did offer back a single cigarette and I look forward to stuffing his mosquitoed corpse into the turret of the Sherman where, after all, it belongs. Gritting our teeth, once more we step inside. The mosquitoes relish the cream and a party of tourists leaps and twists through the museum lashing the air and lunging like blood-crazed marines.

The museum contains spectacular photographic records of the fighting, of the militia units arriving on the scene, and of prisoners being harangued and interrogated by Castro. Advance parachute units dropped by the invaders to cut off Castro's internal supply routes had remained beleaguered, with the main seaborne landing force bogged down by initially hesitant militia units, who considerably overestimated enemy strength and armament. Whether things would have turned out differently had the invasion force managed to knock out Castro's tiny but destructive airforce

* Translated by Claudia Beck.

remains a moot point. One doubts it: the whole Cuban people had been trained and mobilized for defence. Today the task of invading Cuba would be truly formidable in the face of an army of two hundred thousand (the largest in Latin America), based on an obligatory military service of two and a half to three years for every able-bodied male, with a nucleus of forty thousand regulars and equipped with three hundred tanks, a hundred and sixty-five combat planes and twenty-four surface-to-air missile installations. (The Minister for Defence is Fidel's brother, Raúl Castro.) As I have mentioned before, something of the same spirit prevails in Cuba as in Israel—a total commitment to defence born of the commitment to survival. But the parallel cannot be pushed too far: whereas a whole people, a race, is at risk in Israel, the disputed terrain in Cuba is a social system. I doubt whether the Cuban airforce matches the Israeli one in combat efficiency, and, of course, the army has not yet been tested in battle. Hopefully, it will never need to be.

In the museum, old soldiers all, we watch fascinated as Carlos brings an electronic, stage-by-stage map of the battle to life. Afterwards, we wander down to the beach. Small boys are leaping off a jetty into the sea. I sit on the rocks trying to imagine what it was like, the grinding of machines, the wading ashore, the cries of the wounded, the snarl of gunfire. In the museum there is a chart classifying the invading force by civilian occupation, the burden of the argument being that the majority were proprietors of some sort. I don't know, it may be so, but clearly many of them were of fairly humble background and, much as I opposed their venture, I cannot accept the official Cuban refusal to grant them even a modicum of courage, of sincerity. A novelist finds it difficult to sustain a Manichean view of the world. Someone should remind our poet that even Batista's soldiers had mothers somewhere, conceivably many of them humbler in status than his own.

'Now,' says Carlos, 'let us proceed from one kind of crocodile to another.'

Climbing the steps of the coach for perhaps the fiftieth time, past Rafael's benign greeting, 'Eming-way', I notice that the windows are clouding over again. But the spunk has gone, I'm making no more trouble. On the way to the crocodile farm, Carlos explains that in the old days hunters had almost eliminated the species, but the Revolution was committed to preserving Cuba's natural wildlife and history. We walk along a rutted path to a swampy expanse of water larger than a pond, but smaller than a lake, where, behind a wire fence four feet high, twenty thousand scaly logs of all sizes are lying shoulder to shoulder (if that is the phrase) in a state of deceptive lethargy. In such slum conditions, in so overcrowded a watery tenement, finding a mate is presumably no problem, but feeding time must be a lively scene. Rafael assures the Old Swiss that the crocs always sleep it off in mid-afternoon and there is no danger in jumping over the fence. Picking up a bundle of dry leaves, I toss them into the water, sparking off a dreadful, convergent rush of snapping jaws. Those with movie cameras so appreciate this bit of effects-work that I am soon permanently employed in one of the film industry's most humble roles. As someone who dislikes washing dishes, I have always bemoaned man's enslavement to his stomach; but these elongated creatures live to eat, they are all stomach. On the other hand, they don't have to wash dishes.

Carlos: 'You know why they keep their jaws permanently open?'

'In the hope of a bird flying in?'

'So they say.'

A boat trip; a canal cut through swampland leading to a huge lake in which a narrow channel of navigable water is marker-buoyed between thickets of reeds. A large wooden platform erected on stilts in the middle of the lake constitutes the headquarters and siesta retreat of workers dredging the shallow waters. The sun is cruelly bright and Monsieur Lepinay sprawls on the boat's upper, exposed deck, naked, intoxicated. After half an hour we come to a new holiday village built on stilts and modelled on Indian dwellings of the pre-Columbus period. Life-scale models of Indian hunters, fishermen, and children greet us at the approach to this impressive technical achievement with its telephone, wireless and cable services, its bar, restaurant, and tourists' boutique. But it must have been expensive to build, and the mosquitoes at night are beyond contemplation.

And so we retreat from the Bay of Pigs, past placards urging solidarity among guerrillas, posters honouring the Communist Party, and notices announcing that a local Party chieftain has just joined a volunteer brigade. After a night in the Hotel Deauville we head out of Havana again, westwards, through the north-coast port of Meriel with its fishing school perched on a hill and its large cement factory striving vainly to meet Cuba's needs, and into the province of Pinar del Río (Pines of the River). Passing the long Sierra del Rosario and the town of San Cristóbal, the countryside assumes unexpected eccentricities, suggesting to my untutored eye the meridional rather than the tropical. The wooded hillsides remind me of the French Midi, but there are also fairytale sugar-loaf hillocks of rock straight out of a Dürer engraving, dragon's baubles which no knight-errant could resist. We see now our first freight-train and then, abruptly, we are into the tobacco country.

Two weeks ago, soon after our arrival, we visited the Partagas tobacco factory in Havana where rows of workers, male and female, black and white, sit in apparent contentment at long tables moulding cigars out of tobacco leaves with agile, sensitive fingers. A lovely place, warm with smiles and a quiet pride. The director introduces us collectively, announces our several nationalities, and the workers then bang their tables in appreciation. In a basement old men, ripe with wisdom and cunning, are sorting out the large tobacco leaves by size and quality; the seductive aroma banishes all thought of nicotine and cancer. For a smoker who well knows the cost, the luxury, of a single good cigar in his own country, the sight of freshly bound cigars lying about in huge, carefree heaps produces a giddy sensation, as if he had suddenly stepped through the curtain of a dream-harem where the most gorgeous creatures of Saudi Arabia were lying about in tantalizing untouchability. The Young Swiss, needless to say, steps straight forward and picks up several assorted cigars, sniffs them as if he were an important foreign buyer sceptical of their quality, then pockets them with an expression hinting that he might later consent to order a few hundred thousand if they give satisfaction. A more delicate strategy is to approach a worker of the opposite sex and to gaze in awe, wonder, and longing at their magic fingers; such attention invariably produces a shy smile and a brace of cigars. (Alas, contrary to legend, the girls don't roll the cigars on their thighs.) But the nicest thing about Partagas is the blending of efficiency with informality—it being the school holidays, several mothers have brought their children to work, and these children are neither subdued nor a nuisance. In fact, the introduction of female workers to cigar-making is a comparatively recent phenomenon; a mural dating from 1945 depicts an all-male workforce (virtually all-white too) whose aspirations to respectability could scarcely be exceeded by a group of Dutch burghers posing for Rembrandt. At the end of our visit we are all formally presented with a medium-sized cigar and a large variety of colourful Partagas labels. The Young Swiss, volunteering to accept cigars on behalf of those who do not smoke, is firmly told by an exasperated Carlos to take it easy.

The tobacco country of Pinar del Río is charming, dotted as it is with large, red wooden storehouses shaped like Dutch barns and showing a few tiny windows in the roof. (To retain the essential moisture, tobacco is hung from high bars in the dark.) Although only about twenty per cent of Cuban agriculture remains in private hands (farms of up to a hundred acres), as much as eighty per cent of tobacco farming is private. I ask Carlos why this is so, and he replies that it is not policy to nationalize all lands, only the great *latifundia*. But the real reason, I suspect, is that the skilled and specialized nature of tobacco-growing dictates that it be entrusted to experienced and profit-seeking hands.

We disembark at an experimental tobacco station where research vital to the national economy is conducted with the aid of the latest Soviet, German, and British instruments for gauging humidity, temperature changes and seed potential. Two technicians lead us into a kind of schoolroom housing a blackboard and a collection of specialized treatises on tobacco. Offering us black coffee, they amiably invite questions. As a pipe-smoker I am nursing one big question: what is the matter with Cuban pipe tobacco? In the Soviet Union I bought a cardboard box of tobacco which roasted my tongue, scorched my throat and generally burned up like a pile of dry leaves on a summer's day. A box of Cuban tobacco I purchased in Havana proved to be slightly less like sawdust, but not much; it, too, burned rather than smoked, leaving the tongue raw. So now, in the friendliest possible spirit, and observed with dour suspicion by Nicole, I present the technicians (a) with the dusty remains of my Cuban tobacco and (b) with a tin of Virginian tobacco purchased in London and still moist despite long exposure to a tropical climate.

A conference in Spanish ensues which I cannot follow. I suspect that my London tin will be carried away for unimaginable interrogations, tests, and tortures, do I not plead that it alone guarantees the happiness of my few remaining days in Cuba. One technician then explains that

Virginian is 'different' from Cuban tobacco, thus implying that it is simply a matter of taste, of habit. I point out that Cuba would not dream of selling or exporting dried-out cigars liable to burn rather than smoke. This is agreed. Could it be that the fault lies in the packaging? We depart with this question unresolved.

Once again we are lodged in paradise—a new hotel of concrete cabins set round an Olympic pool and framed by Dürer's little hills crested with pine. The pool even has water in it and Monsieur Lepinay has made his swallow dive almost before Rafael has applied the handbrake. But now a grinding boredom besieges Martha and me; we have packed and unpacked our suitcases once too often, and even the flood-lighting at night fails to enchant us. Honeymoon couples wander around forlornly holding hands, stunned by their freedom from toil and the discovery that there is not, after all, anything more to say. Meanwhile, a hearty delegation of Peruvian miners, men without women as Eming-way would say, are drinking beer cheerfully at the bar and moving back and forth to the 'Caballeros' in an unending stream of irrigation.

The presence of these men means one thing: Cuba is desperately trying to break out of its isolation and is prepared to make friends even with a ruling military junta, such as now prevails in Peru, provided its posture towards the United States is hostile. In July 1960 Castro, remembering Bolívar, called on Latin Americans enslaved by the *hacienda*, the great estates which isolate the peasantry and hold them under conservative, pacifying influences from the cradle to the grave, to make of the Andes the Sierra Maestra of the entire continent. But this is easier said than done. In Guatemala the left-wing régime of Jacobo Arbenz, having nationalized certain installations and embarked upon genuine land reform, was snuffed out with American military assistance in 1954. Although Castro has always enjoyed overwhelming popularity in Latin America, and although in the early years Cuban delegations were warmly received throughout the continent, the United States deals with Governments rather than peoples. Admittedly some of these Governments showed signs of bowing to popular sentiment; in 1961 President López Mateos of Mexico felt obliged to defend Cuba and to offer land-distribution gestures of his own, while President Quadros of Brazil decided to strengthen his own domestic popularity by visiting Cuba and decorating Guevara. But American pressure within the Organization of American States was inexorably applied until, in January 1962, the Organization was dragooned into the expulsion of Cuba by a vote of fourteen to six. Even so, it declined to join in sanctions; memories of popular fury after the Bay of Pigs were too fresh.

For his part, Castro widened the breach by roasting the Latin American régimes which had succumbed to American pressure. 'They contend, in their frenzy, that Cuba exports revolutions. There is room for the idea in their commercial, sleepless, and pawnbroker minds, that revolutions can be bought or sold, rented, loaned, exported or imported as one more commodity.' He described the Inter-American Defense Council as 'the nest wherein the most reactionary and pro-Yankee officers of the Latin American armies are hatched.' As for the United States, it traded with Latin America 'like the first Spanish conquerors, who exchanged mirrors and trinkets with the Indians for silver and gold ... To hold on to this torrent of wealth ... to exploit its long-suffering peoples: this is what is hidden behind the military pacts...'

He promised that guerrilla warfare would finally triumph, and in 1966, at the Tricontinental Conference in Havana, he called for violent revolution throughout Latin America. Such a posture naturally intensified Cuba's isolation; the 1968 Cultural Congress in Havana, for example, was attended by sixty-six delegates from France but only seventy-five from the whole of Latin America and the Caribbean (not counting Cuba). Mexico maintained diplomatic relations, but grudgingly. Allende's accession to power was therefore a breakthrough, and Castro promptly accepted Allende's invitation to make a three-week tour of Chile. Cuba was learning that she could achieve more by diplomacy and wooing than by violence and rhetoric; she had, after all, been powerless to prevent the American-inspired ousting of the neutralist President of Brazil, Joao Goulart, in April 1964, and his replacement by the fascistic military régime of Castelo Branco and Costa e Silva. And she was powerless again when President Johnson despatched twenty-seven thousand troops to the Dominican Republic in April 1965, to prevent the return to power of a constitutionally elected non-Communist President, Juan Bosch, whose crime was his willingness to do business with Dominican Communists. And so Castro gratefully accepted the hand held out by Chile, Peru, and, most recently, by the new Peronist régime in the Argentine, the possible implication of this being that the Cuban Press will no longer denounce the repression of Argentinian revolutionaries and the Cuban Government will no longer welcome the Argentinian fugitives whose release from prison is bargained against the lives of hostages. Meanwhile, Panama is courted and the Cuban propaganda machine calls ceaselessly for the independence of Puerto Rico; an August 1972 vote by the UN Decolonization Committee recognizing Puerto Rico as a *colony* provoked exultant comment in the Cuban Press.

Tonight our evening meal has a bizarre climax. Over coffee, a waiter brings round a tray of cigarettes and cigars— an after-dinner treat at reduced prices. The gesture implies a statute of self-limitation: two cigars at most, one packet of cigarettes. But Madame Bourgeois has sniffed a bargain in the wind and her narrow eyes are dancing like the beaks of birds in a patch of worms. 'How much? How much?'

she croaks as the waiter moves slowly round the table. When he reaches her chair and bends forward politely, the loaded tray resting on the palm of his hand, Madame Bourgeois sinks her claws into the gleaming heap and drags it on to the table down to the last cigar, the last cigarette. Silence reigns; the waiter, dumbfounded, looks imploringly to Carlos; but he is out of his depth and even Rafael is at a loss for words. Madame Bourgeois is no fool; conscious of our undivided attention, she is equally aware of our thoughts. But she has the courage of those who have not long to live; when she comes to the eye of the needle and applies for her last apartment, what heavenly judge would allow our poor opinion (envy) of her to outweigh her generosity to her nephews and nieces? Therefore, she loudly instructs the waiter to bring another loaded tray. Carlos his voice cracking, whispers 'Enough, please.' Shrugging, she plunges her hand into her purse and brings out a French banknote the size of a napkin. The shaken waiter rocks on his heels and we drift away to our bedrooms in silence, aware that a comedy has touched the sticky edge of obscenity. Madame Bourgeois reminds us what we could all quite easily become. If we had her wealth. And which of us would refuse it?

But such morbid thoughts may emanate from the bowels. Your narrator lies pathetically on his bed throughout the following day, dragging himself at ten-minute intervals to the toilet with bent back, ashen face, and shuffling feet. Bravely he allows his wife to stroke his burning forehead and to bring him a bowl of clear chicken soup. With a noble 'I'll be all right', he sends her off to inspect a grotto and what may well be the highest waterfall in Pinar del Río. A pain scorches his throat and a stone swells under his chin. So far from home, poor chap, he announces that he only wishes to make it back to his English garden. *Machismo* stoically suppressed, he allows his wife to carry all the suitcases to the coach, totters on her arm, and, once in the coach, collapses his head into her lap. (But this proves rather uncomfortable and he sits up straight.) Vaguely he is aware that Rafael, passing a bottle from mouth to mouth in a Cuban farewell, is dancing the cha-cha in the aisle of the coach, clapping his hands, and waggling his hips before a sceptical Madame Bourgeois. Coming upon our narrator, Rafael expresses concern: 'Eming-way not good?' But the firewater within the bottle will surely cure me. I am ashamed to put it to my lips, for these have suddenly been cracked, crusted, poisoned, and yellowed by the sun. The pinkish cream I apply to my mouth softens the skin but merely retards the inevitable formation of new reptilian scales. I look, as my aunt used to say, very poorly.

The Last of Havana

We are back at the Deauville Hotel. The same spotless room with its jug of iced water nods to us with bored familiarity, declining to divulge what other guests it has entertained in the interval. Surveying my pathetic form sprawled upon the bed in helpless debility, Martha concludes that I should see a doctor. Well, *mañana* to that as to everything else. 'I'm sorry,' I murmur bravely and fall into a harassed sleep. *Mañana* does indeed bring signs of recovery; although my lips continue to resemble volcanic lava, certain pains, fevers, and lumps have definitely abated.

Heading out of Havana to visit the new Lenin Park, I notice how many baseball pitches, athletics tracks, and basketball courts line the suburban roads. The régime is dedicated to fitness-through-recreation and in 1961 created a Ministry of Physical Education to ensure that the whole able-bodied population became equally dedicated. The crucial relationship with the Soviet bloc has led to an emphasis on sports widely popular throughout the world—notably, soccer, athletics, and gymnastics—but it is baseball (*beisbol*) which remains the popular passion. The fortunes of leading American teams are still followed keenly, whatever national poet Guillén may think about it. It will be some years before the archetypal Cuban heroes cease to be the boxer, the base-ball star, the guerrilla, and the super cane-cutter.

Situated some thirty minutes from Central Havana, the Lenin Park proves to be less diverting than Disneyland, but less crass. Here the sedate, responsible, healthy socialist ethic is reflected in an artificial lake for boating and aquatic displays, children's playgrounds, Saturday rodeos, and a delicately designed circular aquarium. All for the family. I feel tired. Mounting the coach, I cannot even respond with the routine grin to Rafael's monotonous greeting.

Havana, of course, was formerly one of the world's great emporia of vice and prostitution, but such sports are mainly the provinces of the rich and the foreign, and I doubt whether more than a handful of Cubans still remaining in Cuba regret their demise. Nevertheless, an arresting spectacle (on our return) is a Saturday morning crowd, predominantly male, gathered on La Rampa to gaze intently through a curved window at seven models parading costumes. (One of the models is a man, but he excites practically no interest at all.) Accompanied by muzak, each pretty girl executes a set-piece promenade along a curving ramp, comes right up to the window, turns, pirouettes, and retreats daintily. By the time her six companions have done their thing (and the pace is inexorable) she must be ready to step out from the wings in a new costume. Dresses, miniskirts, trouser suits, the lot. Wouldn't turn a crowd on Fifth Avenue wild but we aren't on Fifth Avenue. The girls are heavily made-up, with a lot of eye-shadow, and their faces are rigidly impassive. Clearly, the crowd of gently jostling men is not composed of apprentice couturiers or good husbands wondering whether their wives deserve something special. An odd scene, really, reminding me vaguely of the brothel-streets of northern Europe where the men walk up and down examining the human commodities seated in neon-lit windows like half-dressed waxworks from Madame Tussaud's. A Western fashion show, by contrast, is deliberately sexless, the clothes are everything, and the select audience is composed of buyers, trades-people, fashion editors, and photographers. But in all probability the magnetism of the display on La Rampa is not exclusively sexual—it provides a splash of colour, of glamour, in a context of austerity.

Certainly the Castro régime has persistently exhorted the Revolutionary male to abandon his inherited bad habits. The abolition of prostitution was simultaneously a blow to the profit motive and a gesture to the dignity of women. But at grass-roots level the campaign for female equality is an uphill struggle. The cult of *machismo*, or male prowess, retains its old hold, ar.d it is not easy for someone like Fidel, who according to Cuban lore embodies *machismo* to a high degree, to preach it down. The true *macho* is a fellow who tests and proves his manhood by means of a well-groomed appearance, eloquence, wit, splendid gestures, a zest for action, physical courage, and self-confidence. But there is one further ingredient: the head of his bed must be covered with notches. The question then arises as to whether Casanova can ever truly respect women. It is not, of course, the case that a man inhibited by religious or other forms of monogamous morality necessarily respects women, nor is it true that a man who has no shame about fornication or adultery necessarily does not. The doubt arises where the pursuit of the attractive female becomes a form of big-game hunting, with female 'virtue' accorded the status of a tiger's head.

Cuban society has reflected most of the paternalism so dear to Spain. Even after marriage a woman remains a member of her father's family, to whose name she adds her husband's. Yet the régime has encouraged formal civil marriage, not only because it offers children a more stable environment, but also because it affords women more protection than the common-law marriages so prevalent in rural

Cuba before the Revolution. (Hence the old proverbial peasant explanation, 'I am single and here is my wife.') In the first year of the Revolution at least four hundred thousand couples are said to have formalized their marriages. Due largely to the relative weakness of the Church's influence even in pre-Revolutionary Cuba, divorce has generally been accepted with little or no stigma attached. But even today contraception is doubtful: 'sometimes yes, sometimes no', Carlos tells me, wishing I hadn't mentioned it.

Castro has spoken of a revolution within the Revolution, the emancipation of women (whose equality of rights, incidentally, is guaranteed by the Fundamental Law of 1959). 'I believe,' he said, 'that in reality all of us are prejudiced in regard to women.' The poor woman, he argues, has been doubly exploited: by her poverty, and by male prejudice from within her own class. The woman is like the black: she suffers twice over. Only the socialist Revolution, Castro insists, can wipe out sexual and racial discrimination.

The Federation of Cuban Women is both a Communist and a feminist organization. It was founded in August 1960 with the aims of increasing the number of women employed in wage work, of organizing day-care centres for children, sanitary brigades, and public health campaigns, and generally of harnessing women to those areas of economic and social activity where they are most needed or useful. (Women workers pay a proportion of their wages to cover the expenses of the day nurseries, although women engaged in agricultural production are apparently exempt.)

Officially, there is now a reverse discrimination policy designed to redress the imbalance: any available job which can be performed by either sex must be given to the female applicant. There are women hospital directors and school directors, women's tractor brigades, and women's units to run calf-farms. Women are particularly active in the Committees for the Defence of the Revolution, and the young girls, as part of their militia training, learn how to fire a rifle. Today, one sees in the countryside groups of schoolgirls who are poised, assured, and liberated from an aboriginal sense of dispossession.

Nearly fifty per cent of university students are female. At the University of Oriente, in Santiago, women constitute ninety per cent of the students of education, fifty per cent of medical students, and thirty per cent of those studying engineering. Over half the members of the Union of Young Communists are women, although there is only one woman in the Central Committee of the Party. Paradoxically, women have yet to make a breakthrough in the one field which a European or an American might assume would present the fewest obstacles—literature; of forty poets represented in a recent anthology of Cuban poetry, only two are women, and both of those very young.

Tonight we are promised a special treat, a quick taste of the old corruption, a visit to the famous Tropicana nightclub. So depressing ultimately is the impact of regular set meals in pre-determined company that we all look forward to the Tropicana with childlike excitement, even though the meals and the company will remain as pre-determined as ever. In the Deauville bar Martha makes the point to Carlos how nice it would have been if a few of us could just once have eaten an evening meal in a restaurant of our choice.

Carlos nods. 'Quite so. But do you realize how much it would cost you?'

We ask him how much.

'In a lower grade popular restaurant, five pesos per person. In a better restaurant, ten, fifteen, even twenty pesos a head.'

'Can ordinary Cubans afford such prices?'

'Not every day. For special occasions, yes. People now

have money in their pockets and there is not so much to spend it on.'

'Presumably the Soviet technicians eat quite frequently in such restaurants?'

Carlos shrugs his perennial shrug. 'Don't ask me; I don't move in such circles.'

'Élite circles?'

'There is no élite in Cuba, please. By now you should have recognized that.'

'Do you think that people are becoming discontented about the lack of consumer goods?'

'Some people grumble. Most people just hope things will improve. But everyone understands the difficulties.'

Perhaps they do; but it is my impression that what the Cuban people will pretty soon demand on pain of serious disaffection is an economy which works. In certain vital respects the Cuban one doesn't. Not, I think, because of 'socialism'. One does well to remember that the pre-Revolutionary bourgeoisie in Cuba was generally more parasitical than productive, plundering the national wealth rather than enhancing it. In a direct sense the country gained more than it lost by expropriating the land, real estate, and services previously owned by this class. But the side-effects of rapid and determined socialization, whether in Cuba or Chile, inevitably constitute a threat to economic viability. Two such effects stand out: the withdrawal of foreign investments and the loss of skilled, experienced personnel, both native and foreign. Some form of economic embargo is also to be expected.

In Cuba, the young idealists who inherited power in January 1959 obviously knew precious little about how to run an economy. They had ideas, of course, and when those ideas failed they tried others, like eccentric sea captains constantly urging their crews to turn full circle in pursuit of an invisible white whale. One example, already noted, was the early emphasis on diversification, followed by an almost manic concentration on the sugar crop alone. Castro's attitude towards money and material incentives is another case in point. He and Guevara, sharing a Utopian contempt for money and a Utopian impatience to hurry along the Communist day when each would be rewarded according to his needs, at first urged Cubans to find ethical imperatives for rolling up their sleeves. But the old Communists of the Popular Socialist Party were sceptical and, as they gained influence, injected into the labour force Soviet-style material incentives and privileges on the Stakhanovite model of pay for productivity. Then Castro grew furious, alluded to growing popular resentments, made local telephone calls free (up to three minutes), and once again began to denounce money. As a consequence, everyone began to volunteer to do everyone else's work for nothing while being paid for not doing their own work.

Yet an impressive welfare state did emerge; the under-privileged peasantry was indeed treated like an aristocracy; and, although René Dumont reports that life has become too plushy for army officers, top officials, and representatives of Alfa Romeo, one can safely say that Cuba has not yet begun to develop the 'new class' of well-heeled managers and administrators so conspicuous in Eastern Europe and the Soviet Union.

The volunteer-work principle has much to recommend it morally and socially, attempting as it does in Chinese style to close the stratification gap between 'hand workers' and 'head workers' or, in American terms, between white- and blue-collar workers. And some of its achievements are impressive, notably the 'cordon' of orange groves, coffee plantations, and dairy farms stretching round Havana. But the division of labour, with its concomitant specializations and skills, is, like it or not, an irreversible ingredient of modern economic efficiency. As Dumont puts it, when a group of twenty-six members of the Union of Artists and Writers sets off on a Wednesday to cut cane, they break the day with a pleasant picnic and cut about a quarter of the cane that a comparable group of professionals would harvest. Added to this, production statistics tell a disappointing tale. In 1967 cement production was more or less static at the 1960 level; in the same period the amount of cement imported increased from four thousand to two hundred and seventy-seven thousand tons. By 1967 Cuba's trade deficit was almost one million dollars per day.

In fairness, the country is held back by factors beyond the control of any government. For one thing, the population is small (although larger than Denmark's). Soil and climatic conditions greatly reduce the natural productivity of cattle. Whereas in France one hundred head of cattle yield on average 7.3 tons of meat and a hundred and twenty-two tons of milk, in Cuba the corresponding figures are 2.7 tons and eleven tons. Castro has imported pedigree foreign bulls, but it takes three years from the start of artificial insemination before the first cross-bred cows come into milk. Nor is Cuba at all rich in mineral resources.

Laziness and absenteeism are factors which cannot be discounted. On the contrary, they have provoked more than one angry harangue from Castro. In March 1968 he chided Cubans for being heroic at crucial moments, but lacking in consistency and perseverance. Naturally, he did not blame these failings on socialism, which proponents of free enterprise and the profit motive invariably do. Instead, he blamed the mentality of 'underdevelopment'. Probably he is right. It is said, and seems to be proved, that German workers work harder and more productively than British workers; well, in both countries most of them are employed by private firms. In the same way, the average East German worker outstrips his Polish colleague; yet both work within a socialist system. As for the 'profit motive', how many Western employees does it directly touch? Certainly not those millions of white-collar men and women who are daily sucked into banks, insurance offices, and the clerical divisions of giant corporations. They drudge away for a fixed salary; at the end of the year, with a bit of luck, they'll drudge for two hundred and fifty dollars more. No, as the example of the two Germanies demonstrates, work, hard work, persistent work, is an ethic deeply seeded in a national culture and its particular historical development.

Wearing our very best clothes (such as have survived the constant packing and unpacking in wearable order) we climb out of the coach and hurry excitedly towards the entrance of the Tropicana, which is situated in a garden suburb. A cheerful party of insurance workers (Carlos explains) celebrating a wedding are jostling with attendants at the door, while other natives, lacking tickets, queue glumly under the palm trees. A couple of big black Buicks in the driveway prompt the thought that the Ambassador of Sierra Leone is already within, bearing witness to the immense social, cultural, etc., etc. advances made by etc. One of Havana's few remaining nightclubs, the Tropicana costs twenty-five pesos a head (including a set dinner, fairly vile) for individual patrons, and fifteen pesos for parties like ours. Times have changed, but something of the old aura, the brash glitter, lingers on; wall photographs of George Raft, Carmen Miranda, Betty Grable, Errol Flynn, and Frank Sinatra blessing Cuba with their charms bear witness to a golden age when the life of Havana began at dusk. And the waiters still sport white coats and black ties, though the bottles of beer they carry on their trays must remind them of times when bottles of champagne, scotch, and brandy were paid for in dollar bills with a casual 'keep the change'. The rumbas and sambas which throb continuously are probably much what they once were, but the couples on the dance floor are now casually dressed and include their fair share of blacks. It is the epic floorshow, the cabaret itself, which bears the most powerful tribute to the enduring impact of Hollywood in the era of de Mille and Goldwyn, an erotic-spectacular set in Ancient Rome with leggy slave-girls, spectacular costume-changes, floodlit gladiators, glinting sequins, a song-a-minute, and a succession of Caesar's wives, whose antics with a chiffon gown put them squarely within range of suspicion. Two hours of it; what more can you ask?

A visit to the theatre completes our planned itinerary. The company is that of the National Theatre, the play is Bertholt Brecht's *Days of the Commune* (about the Paris Commune of 1871), and the director has come all the way from the East German Berliner Ensemble. (Also highly regarded in Havana are El Teatro Nacional de Guiñol and the Ballet de Cuba, founded in 1948 by the ballerina Alicia Alonso.) Judging by the rows of empty seats, the legitimate theatre is less than a passion in Havana; only a squad of schoolgirls in beige blouses and a motley bunch of travel-scarred tourists from the Deauville Hotel save the day. Action is apparently what the younger members of the audience desire; when Brecht's Communards engage in lengthy debates there is a noisy emptying of the stalls behind us, though the beige schoolgirls, no doubt under the watchful eye of a teacher, stay put. At the end of the play the desperate Communards, whose struggle against Thiers and Bismarck should surely carry some relevance to modern Cubans, aim their rifles from behind the barricades and fire off salvoes of blanks. At this the young audience bursts into laughter and cheers derisively. I've no idea why.

'Well,' says Carlos in the coach, 'thank you very much. We have showed you all we can of Cuba and I hope you have enjoyed your holiday here. For my part, it has been a great pleasure to share your journey.'

With one voice—a bit ragged—we thank Carlos. For

everything. And Rafael. And Pedro. Rafael writes down the names and addresses of a few passengers privileged to have caught his imagination, all of them female. My wife heads the list—Señora Eming-way. He promises to visit us in London, and then gives me an indescribable wink. 'Good fell-ow.'

But our time has not yet run out. Tomorrow it was to be the house, now a museum, of the real Eming-way, but the key is with the Old Man or the Sea, so it's more Have Not than Have. We agree to spend the remainder of our time in a leisurely re-exploration of the National Museum, with particular regard to the fine arts. And so with a new confidence we tread the sidewalks, passing many a staring citizen who has seen much less of the island of Cuba than we—yet knows so much more.

There is no entrance fee. We halt in the main courtyard or patio to examine some large iron statues of abstract-modernist design. Next, a display of posters, some political, some promoted by the tourist industry. Then, a room called Sala Didactica, which I wrongly assume refers to politically committed art, but which in reality exhibits the basic techniques and processes employed by lithographers, caligraphers, and engravers.

We climb a ramp to the first floor. Here begins an exhibition of Cuban painting, arranged chronologically. The eighteenth-century pictures are much of a muchness, all post-Rubens frill, flush, and flounce, but one canvas does pull me up short. In a crowded market-place a bull has broken loose and is bearing down on a Junoesque lady who, skirts riding high up her thighs, sprawls on her back expecting the worst.

We arrive at the twentieth century. Here, in the early years, the influence of European post-impressionism is strong. Wilfredo Lam, a half-Chinese, half-Negro artist born in 1902, who returned to Cuba from Europe during the

Second World War, seems to have been in perpetual pursuit of Picasso. By the turn of the century Cuban art had made a definitive break with realism and classicism; the effects of this are still in evidence.

So, indeed, a notice posted at the entrance to the post-Revolutionary rooms warns us. To my mind it is an astonishing and unique feature of the Cuban Revolution, this pride in the marriage of the socialist ethic with expressionism, cubism, surrealism, pop and op, and all the other motions in the surging choreography of modern art. To visit Cuba is to witness at every turn examples of a cheerful, fresh visual ingenuity—witness only the designs and carvings inlaid on the paving stones of La Rampa. How long it will last and why visiting Soviet technicians have not yet frowned it out of existence I do not know.

Cuban post-Revolutionary art is quite something. As in great periods of religiously inspired painting, every artist seems to be his own master while aware of a binding force presiding over his efforts and joining him to an experience larger than his canvas. Unfortunately, words enjoy little power to convey the visual; the more doggedly they attempt to catch and define the disparate elements of a design, the more they overwhelm the reader with a plethora of details which obscure more than they reveal. So let me merely mention:

An expressionist woodcut, 'Carrera de bicicletas' (1961), by Lesbia Vart Dumois; the robust realism of 'Milicias campesinas' (1961), by Serrando Cabrera Moreno; the work of Sandu Darie; the pop art of Raúl Martínez; the collages of Antonio Vidal, who employs both paint and fabrics; the fusion of op art with political commitment in Alfredo Sosabravo's 'Regresando de Indochina' (1967); and the huge 'El Tercio Mundo' (1965) by Wilfredo Lam, a widescreen of white figures on a green background strongly reminiscent of Picasso's *Guernica*. I would happily continue with this list, out of gratitude to the many Cuban artists whose work makes the eye sit up and dance.

Martha and I are determined, fanatically determined, to buy a few lithographs by contemporary artists. At the entrance to the National Museum a half-dozen are for sale, but none of them is by an artist we particularly admire and none is in colour. It seems to us that Cuban art is colour or it is nothing. So we ask the girl, in a fairly resolute display of Spanish, where in town one can buy such things. She shrugs. She consults a janitor. He shrugs. We hurry back to the Deauville, run into Carlos, and consult him. He telephones his employers and emerges with the answer. (Good old Carlos.) So off we go, winding through the old colonial town, greatly aided by a map we have coaxed out of the sky, heading for the old San Francisco convent down by the harbour, opposite to the customs shed.

At the street door we are questioned by a porter. He makes an internal telephone call. We wait in a small room. A young lady whose style immediately strikes me as more Spanish than Cuban comes to fetch us; puts us in an elevator which must have been presented by Columbus on arrival; and finally opens the door on a large room filled with the most amazing bric-a-brac—candlesticks, family portraits, china dogs, porcelain shepherdesses, coral necklaces, snuff boxes, riding crops, you name it. Were our sense of mission not so obsessive, we would gladly spend an hour browsing through this enchanting junk, and would probably convince ourselves in the end that we need nothing so much as a really sympathetic Mother and Child for the dining-room wall. We explain to Señorita Madrid that we are hunting for contemporary Cuban art.

'Then this is not the place.'

Merde.

'Could you please tell us where is the place?'

She doesn't know, sorry.

'Could you *possibly* find out?'

Difficult.

'Someone else in the building might know? The Director, for example.'

'He is busy.'

'Perhaps you could make a phone call ... to La Casa de las Américas ... the Ministry ... somewhere. The Union of Cuban Writers and Artists. Please.'

'Kindly wait here.'

The lady vanishes. She returns. Nothing doing. *Nyet, no, no, nein, non* .... Did she make the phone calls? She says she did. Whom did she phone? Her answer is vague, we are a nuisance, unexpected, irregular. So her sulky expression suggests.

'How do ordinary Cubans obtain lithographs or paintings?'

The idea has never occurred to her. Shrug. Maybe they know the artist.

'There must be some galleries in Havana.'

'Definitely not. But tomorrow some may be open.'

'There are none, but they may be open tomorrow?'

Quite so. Must I repeat everything she says? We don't budge and she obviously has the feeling that if she leaves us alone with the bric-à-brac, not a single porcelain shepherdess will survive. But she does.

'Excuse me, please.'

She is gone longer this time. She returns.

'Unfortunately all the galleries in Havana are closed for repairs.'

'Ah. *All* of them?'

Indefinitely. But paintings are on sale at the Cuban Pavilion on La Rampa. She smiles now.

We know the Pavilion well. We scramble. Map, bus, change buses, walk. We cross Havana at the double.

It looks half-built, the Cuban Pavilion, but this is deliberate, providing as it does ample space for internal building and scaffolding, with slide-away roofs, half-walls and most of the facilities a display artist or exhibition director could want. Unfortunately, it is closed. We walk across to the Havana Libre, don't attempt to buy a drink in the residents-only cafeteria, don't attempt to gather information in the Cubans-only tourist office, but head expertly for the distressed-foreigners-only bureau. It is exactly as we left it three weeks ago; the same five young men and women are idly chatting in identical postures. The girl remembers us.

'You're not still looking for a map?' she laughs.

'Where can we buy pictures?'

'Pictures?'

'Yes. Cuban art. Contemporary.'

'You wish to see Cuban art?'

'To buy it.'

'Have you tried the National Museum?'

'Yes.'

'The San Francisco convent then?'

'Are paintings sold, by any chance, in the Cuban Pavilion?'

A conference ensues. The verdict is no.

'Listen. You are a tourist office and we have come all the way from London to buy one of your fine lithographs. Surely ...'

The girl has a bright idea. She thinks it very possible that we might find what we want by consulting the cultural attaché of the Cuban Embassy in London.

Thank you and goodbye.

Since these are our last hours in Havana, we decide to walk. But we walk in silence. As travellers we are rapidly decomposing.

One day I may write about this trip and I attempt to soak in a last impression. In my experience, there is such a thing as 'the Communist city'. Havana, Santiago, Belgrade, East Berlin, Leipzig, Prague, Moscow, Novosibirsk, they all have certain qualities in common, disparate as such places are in culture and geography. These cities are essentially conurbations where people live, work, and move about. Part dormitory, part sportsground, part school, part hospital, part refectory, Communist cities are proud enough of their museums, libraries, and universities to maintain such buildings in very good order. The streets are generally clean and the interior of the opera house is freshly painted in red and gold with plush velvet seats. But something is missing.

What is missing? Of course, it lies purely in the eye of the beholder. I, myself, greatly admire and value the worthy amenities listed above, and one can scarcely pretend that many Western cities are equally free of litter, filth, pollution, dire poverty, slums, racial hatred, and violence. That is why we call constantly for more planning, more control of speculative building, more green spaces, more welfare, a greater effort to eradicate crime at its social roots. And yet, and yet ... For me, the great city should also be a whore, a hustler, a fixer, a con-man, a pornographer, an entertainer. No progressive with a social conscience can regard Paris as anything but a scandal; but where would he rather be? The life of a city lies in its contrasts; a short walk from the splendours of the Louvre and Notre Dame to a jostling flea market where old books and etchings lie in unruly piles, then a few more steps and a film called *Swedish Nights* beckons, and all the way, at every step, places to eat, to sit down and drink, to watch the world walk past. We may wish to resist corruption in the metropolis, but we also need to be seduced by shop windows, splendid bookstores, magazine stands, shrimp-vendors, and newspapers brimming with lists of things to do, things to see.

The Communist city is not merely the victim of austerity, of the priority of capital investment over consumer goods. It is also a Puritan city, ruled by men who are profoundly distrustful of private pleasures and personal idiosyncrasies, of the bohemian, the hippie, the drunken artist. For these pedagogues and scout-masters, the Western city represents a licence and a licentiousness where everything is permanently Out of Control. To them the thought of epicures and sensual anarchists gathering in darkened cellars to eat foreign foods is an intolerable symbol of chaos welling up from the sewers, from the unregenerate past. Banish Sin. Consequently the Communist city is healthy but barren, whereas the Western city is diseased but fertile. To wander round the Left Bank, or Soho, or Greenwich Village, or the waterfront area of Amsterdam, is to be in communion with human ingenuity operating in severe confines of space. Particularly with regard to food, to restaurants—I keep coming back to that. In the Communist city the restaurant—if you can find it, if you can get in, big ifs—is typically ponderous, sedate, dull, bad. No art, no flair, no real need to please the customer. Cooking is inseparable from private enterprise, and there is no reason at all why a socialist government should not rigorously control the wages, hours of work, and welfare benefits accruing to the cooks, waiters, and cleaners, so long as the boss remains his own master in all other matters.

Of all the cities I have visited, Havana is the one whose mood, style, opportunities, and face have been most radically transformed by Communism.

Still time to kill, a couple of hours. In the boutique we buy a box of twenty-five medium-size cigars for ten dollars, a few books, some travel posters by the artist Hernandez, a bottle of rum, some postcards. (We have sent no postcards back to England on the safe assumption that we would arrive before they did—if they ever did.) Our last meal together is jolly: we are all pleased to be seeing the last of each other; besides, there's no place like home. The Mad Dutchman, whom we haven't seen for three weeks, recounts how he walked ten kilometres somewhere in Oriente to make a rendezvous with a lady who never showed up. Madame Bourgeois is complaining that there is not enough space in her baggage for all her gifts, but she reacts negatively to the suggestion that we carry them for her. Monsieur Lepinay, very brown, talks to me about his hopes for the French Communist Party, hopes which I admit to him I don't entirely share, but he doesn't seem to mind. His wife regards me almost with sympathy now; maybe the Queen will cut my head off when I return. The Old Swiss assesses Cuba as 'a new world to bury the old', and the Young Swiss rejoices to be returning to American Express, Zurich. As for Nicole, she and I have kept our distance since the affair of the dirty windows, which is just as well. Carlos, Rafael, and Pedro have shut themselves off at a separate table as if they could bear no more of it, or us.

After dinner we retire to our rooms to doze for a few hours. In one sense packing for a return journey is easier : you don't have to choose what to take or worry about leaving some life-saving pills behind. On the other hand, one amasses an amazing quantity of awkwardly shaped items which refuse to fit into rectangular suitcases and therefore detach themselves as one more parcel to carry and perhaps lose. Besides, dirty linen always takes up more space than clean.

At midnight, our telephone rings and by one o'clock we have boarded the coach, joined now by the beautiful athletes from Jibacoa who insist on singing. Our last journey through Havana, like our first, is in darkness. But we now recognize the lights, the shapes against the sky, the contours of energy and lethargy which our experiences in this city represent. Sleep well, brave little Cuba, and live long.

Somewhere in this city, a mile away at most, is a man of world stature, a man whose heartbeat is the very clock of the society he has created, led, hectored, and loved. Is he asleep?

We arrive at José Martí Airport three hours before our Ilyushin is due to depart. Emigration formalities, nil. Passports returned. A long queue waits to change its Cuban money, completely valueless beyond the frontier. With a pang of regret I remember my Che Guevara banknote, but I am more preoccupied holding a handkerchief to my suppurating lips.

Carlos waits with us and is suddenly very remote, no longer the man I played chess with in Cienfuegos and Varadero. We erect internal defence mechanisms against the large spaces of the world. We shake hands quickly. 'Adiós.'

Martha sits and reads. Too tired to do either, I wander the empty, closed-down corridors of the airport and come across a small Arrivals and Departures board:

> Madrid–Havana
> Prague –Havana
> Moscow–Havana
> Mexico City–Havana
> Santiago de Chile–Lima–Havana

And that is all.

The Old Swiss has fallen asleep with his head tilted back; Madame Bourgeois with her head tilted forward.

At five-thirty a.m., punctually, an Ilyushin jet of Czechoslovak Airlines takes off from Havana, heads east to avoid the coastline of the United States, then flies north to Newfoundland through a rapidly cooling night.

'They never did return our books, did they?'

But she is already asleep.